Microsoft® Office PowerPoint® 2007

ILLUSTRATED

BRIEF

David Beskeen

COURSE TECHNOLOGY
CENGAGE Learning·

Australia • Brazil • Japan • Korea • Mexico • Singapore • Spain • United Kingdom • United States

COURSE TECHNOLOGY
CENGAGE Learning

Microsoft® Office PowerPoint® 2007—Illustrated Brief

David Beskeen

Senior Acquisitions Editor: Marjorie Hunt

Senior Product Manager: Christina Kling Garrett

Associate Product Manager: Rebecca Padrick

Editorial Assistant: Michelle Camisa

Senior Marketing Manager: Joy Stark

Marketing Coordinator: Jennifer Hankin

Contributing Author: Elizabeth Eisner Reding

Developmental Editor: Rachel Biheller Bunin

Production Editor: Summer Hughes

Copy Editor: Harold Johnson

QA Manuscript Reviewers: Jeff Schwartz, Danielle Shaw, Teresa Storch, Susan Whalen

Cover Designers: Elizabeth Paquin, Kathleen Fivel

Cover Artist: Mark Hunt

Composition: GEX Publishing Services

Proofreader: Cecile Kaufman

Indexer: Alexandra Nickerson

For product information and technology assistance, contact us at
Cengage Learning Customer & Sales Support, 1-800-354-9706

For permission to use material from this text or product, submit all requests online at **cengage.com/permissions**
Further permissions questions can be emailed to
permissionrequest@cengage.com

ISBN-13: 978-1-4239-0523-3

ISBN-10: 1-4239-0523-7

Course Technology
25 Thomson Place
Boston, Massachusetts 02210
USA

Cengage Learning is a leading provider of customized learning solutions with office locations around the globe, including Singapore, the United Kingdom, Australia, Mexico, Brazil, and Japan. Locate your local office at: **international.cengage.com/region**

Cengage Learning products are represented in Canada by Nelson Education, Ltd.

For your lifelong learning solutions, visit **course.cengage.com**

Purchase any of our products at your local college store or at our preferred online store **www.ichapters.com**

Tradmarks:
Some of the product names and company names used in this book have been used for identification purposes only and may be trademarks or registered trademarks of their respective manufacturers and sellers.

Microsoft and the Office logo are either registered trademarks or trademarks of Microsoft Corporation in the United States and/or other countries. Thomson Course Technology is an independent entity from Microsoft Corporation, and not affiliated with Microsoft in any manner.

Credit List

Figure	Credit Line
C-6	Courtesy of Jennifer L. Beskeen
C-12	Courtesy of Barbara Clemens
D-5	Courtesy of Christopher Garrett

Printed in the United States of America
3 4 5 6 7 8 9 11 10 09 08

About This Book

Welcome to *Microsoft Office PowerPoint 2007—Illustrated Brief*! Since the first book in the Illustrated Series was published in 1994, millions of students have used various Illustrated texts to master software skills and learn computer concepts. We are proud to bring you this new Illustrated book on the most exciting version of Microsoft Office ever to release.

As you probably have heard by now, Microsoft completely redesigned this latest version of Office from the ground up. No more menus! No more toolbars! The software changes Microsoft made were based on years of research during which they studied users' needs and work habits. The result is a phenomenal and powerful new version of the software that will make you and your students more productive and help you get better results faster.

Before we started working on this new edition, we also conducted our own research. We reached out to nearly 100 instructors like you who have used previous editions of this book and our Microsoft Office texts. Some of you responded to one of our surveys; others of you generously spent time with us on the phone, telling us your thoughts. Seven of you agreed to serve on our Advisory Board and guided our decisions.

As a result of all the feedback you gave us, we have preserved the features that you love, and made improvements that you suggested and requested. And of course we have covered all the key features of the new software. (For more details on what's new in this edition, please read the Preface.) We are confident that this book and all its available resources will help your students master Microsoft Office PowerPoint 2007.

Advisory Board

We thank our Advisory Board who enthusiastically gave us their opinions and guided our every decision on content and design from beginning to end. They are:

Kristen Callahan, Mercer County Community College

Paulette Comet, Assistant Professor, Community College of Baltimore County

Barbara Comfort, J. Sargeant Reynolds Community College

Margaret Cooksey, Tallahassee Community College

Rachelle Hall, Glendale Community College

Hazel Kates, Miami Dade College

Charles Lupico, Thomas Nelson Community College

Author Acknowledgments

David Beskeen Experience, dedication, hard work, and attention to detail with a little humor thrown in are the qualities of a great editor and Rachel Biheller Bunin is truly a great editor—thank you so much! To all of the professionals at Course Technology, led by Christina Kling Garrett, thanks for your hard work. I would also like to especially thank Marjorie Hunt, who fifteen years ago, gave me my first opportunity to use my knowledge of PowerPoint to help others learn. Finally, a special thanks to my wife, Karen, and the "J's", for always being there.

Preface

Welcome to *Microsoft Office PowerPoint 2007—Illustrated Brief*. If this is your first experience with the Illustrated series, you'll see that this book has a unique design: each skill is presented on two facing pages, with steps on the left and screens on the right. The layout makes it easy to digest a skill without having to read a lot of text and flip pages to see an illustration.

This book is an ideal learning tool for a wide range of learners—the rookies will find the clean design easy to follow and focused with only essential information presented, and the hotshots will appreciate being able to move quickly through the lessons to find the information they need without reading a lot of text. The design also makes this a great reference after the course is over! See the illustration on the right to learn more about the pedagogical and design elements of a typical lesson.

What's New in This Edition

We've made many changes and enhancements to this edition to make it the best ever. Here are some highlights of what's new:

- **New Getting Started with Microsoft Office 2007 Unit**—This unit begins the book and gets students up to speed on features of Office 2007 that are common to all the applications, such as the Ribbon, the Office button, and the Quick Access toolbar.

- **Real Life Independent Challenge**—The new Real Life Independent Challenge exercises offer students the opportunity to create projects that are meaningful to their lives, such as a personal letterhead, a database to track personal expenses, or a budget for buying a house.

- **New Case Study**—A new case study featuring Quest Specialty Travel provides a practical and fun scenario that students can relate to as they learn skills. This

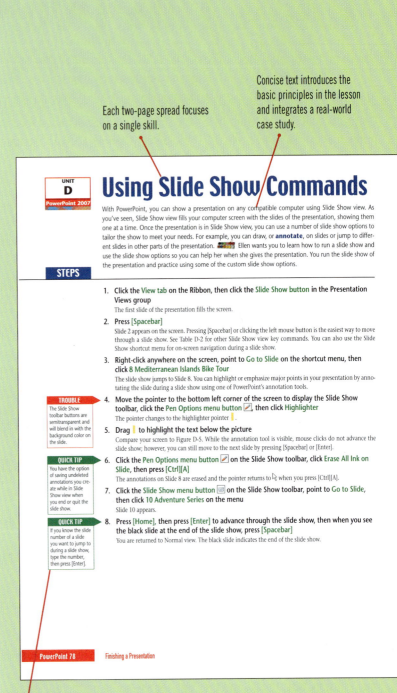

Each two-page spread focuses on a single skill.

Concise text introduces the basic principles in the lesson and integrates a real-world case study.

Hints as well as troubleshooting advice, right where you need it—next to the step itself.

Every lesson features large, full-color representations of what the screen should look like as students complete the numbered steps.

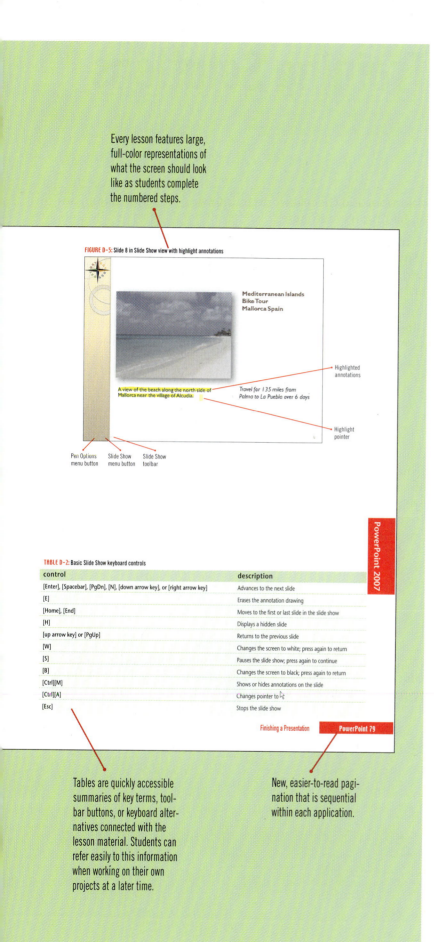

FIGURE D-5: Slide 8 in Slide Show view with highlight annotations

Mediterranean Islands
Bike Tour
Mallorca Spain

A view of the beach along the north side of Mallorca near the village of Alcudia.

Travel for 135 miles from Palma to La Puebla over 6 days

Highlighted annotations

Highlight pointer

Pen Options menu button

Slide Show menu button

Slide Show toolbar

TABLE D-2: Basic Slide Show keyboard controls

control	description
[Enter], [Spacebar], [PgDn], [N], [down arrow key], or [right arrow key]	Advances to the next slide
[E]	Erases the annotation drawing
[Home], [End]	Moves to the first or last slide in the slide show
[H]	Displays a hidden slide
[up arrow key] or [PgUp]	Returns to the previous slide
[W]	Changes the screen to white; press again to return
[S]	Pauses the slide show; press again to continue
[B]	Changes the screen to black; press again to return
[Ctrl][M]	Shows or hides annotations on the slide
[Ctrl][A]	Changes pointer to
[Esc]	Stops the slide show

Tables are quickly accessible summaries of key terms, toolbar buttons, or keyboard alternatives connected with the lesson material. Students can refer easily to this information when working on their own projects at a later time.

New, easier-to-read pagination that is sequential within each application.

fictional company offers a wide variety of tours around the world.

- **Content Improvements**—All of the content in the book has been updated to cover Office 2007 and also to address instructor feedback. See the instructor resource CD for details on specific content changes for PowerPoint.

Assignments

The lessons use Quest Specialty Travel, a fictional adventure travel company, as the case study. The assignments on the light purple pages at the end of each unit increase in difficulty. Data files and case studies provide a variety of interesting and relevant business applications. Assignments include:

- **Concepts Reviews** consist of multiple choice, matching, and screen identification questions.

- **Skills Reviews** provide additional hands-on, step-by-step reinforcement.

- **Independent Challenges** are case projects requiring critical thinking and application of the unit skills. The Independent Challenges increase in difficulty, with the first one in each unit being the easiest. Independent Challenges 2 and 3 become increasingly open-ended, requiring more independent problem solving.

- **Real Life Independent Challenges** are practical exercises in which students create documents to help them with their every day lives.

- **Advanced Challenge Exercises** set within the Independent Challenges provide optional steps for more advanced students.

- **Visual Workshops** are practical, self-graded capstone projects that require independent problem solving.

Assessment & Training Solutions

SAM 2007

SAM 2007 helps bridge the gap between the classroom and the real world by allowing students to train and test on important computer skills in an active, hands-on environment.

SAM 2007's easy-to-use system includes powerful interactive exams, training or projects on critical applications such as Word, Excel, Access, PowerPoint, Outlook, Windows, the Internet, and much more. SAM simulates the application environment, allowing students to demonstrate their knowledge and think through the skills by performing real-world tasks.

Designed to be used with the Illustrated series, SAM 2007 includes built-in page references so students can print helpful study guides that match the Illustrated textbooks used in class. Powerful administrative options allow instructors to schedule exams and assignments, secure tests, and run reports with almost limitless flexibility.

Student Edition Labs

Our Web-based interactive labs help students master hundreds of computer concepts, including input and output devices, file management and desktop applications, computer ethics, virus protection, and much more. Featuring up-to-the-minute content, eye-popping graphics, and rich animation, the highly interactive Student Edition Labs offer students an alternative way to learn through dynamic observation, step-by-step practice, and challenging review questions. Also available on CD at an additional cost.

Online Content   Blackboard

Blackboard is the leading distance learning solution provider and class-management platform today. Course Technology has partnered with Blackboard to bring you premium online content. Instructors: Content for use with *Microsoft Office PowerPoint 2007—Illustrated Brief* is available in a Blackboard Course Cartridge and may include topic reviews, case projects, review questions, test banks, practice tests, custom syllabi, and more.

Course Technology also has solutions for several other learning management systems. Please visit *www.course.com* today to see what's available for this title.

Instructor Resources

The Instructor Resources CD is Course Technology's way of putting the resources and information needed to teach and learn effectively into your hands. With an integrated array of teaching and learning tools that offers you and your students a broad range of technology-based instructional options, we believe this CD represents the highest quality and most cutting edge resources available to instructors today. Many of these resources are available at *www.course.com*. The resources available with this book are:

- **Instructor's Manual**—Available as an electronic file, the Instructor's Manual includes detailed lecture topics with teaching tips for each unit.

- **Sample Syllabus**—Prepare and customize your course easily using this sample course outline.

- **PowerPoint Presentations**—Each unit has a corresponding PowerPoint presentation that you can use in lecture, distribute to your students, or customize to suit your course.

- **Figure Files**—The figures in the text are provided on the Instructor Resources CD to help you illustrate key topics or concepts. You can create traditional overhead transparencies by printing the figure files. Or you can create electronic slide shows by using the figures in a presentation program such as PowerPoint.

- **Solutions to Exercises**—Solutions to Exercises contains every file students are asked to create or modify in the lessons and end-of-unit material. Also provided in this section, there is a document outlining the solutions for the end-of-unit Concepts Review, Skills Review, and Independent Challenges. An Annotated Solution File and Grading Rubric accompany each file and can be used together for quick and easy grading.

- **Data Files for Students**—To complete most of the units in this book, your students will need Data Files. You can post the Data Files on a file server for students to copy. The Data Files are available on the Instructor Resources CD-ROM, the Review Pack, and can also be downloaded from www.course.com. In this edition, we have included a lesson on downloading the Data Files for this book, see page xvi.

Instruct students to use the Data Files List included on the Review Pack and the Instructor Resources CD. This list gives instructions on copying and organizing files.

- **ExamView**—ExamView is a powerful testing software package that allows you to create and administer printed, computer (LAN-based), and Internet exams. ExamView includes hundreds of questions that correspond to the topics covered in this text, enabling students to generate detailed study guides that include page references for further review. The computer-based and Internet testing components allow students to take exams at their computers, and also saves you time by grading each exam automatically.

CourseCasts–Learning on the Go. Always available...always relevant.

Want to keep up with the latest technology trends relevant to you? Visit our site to find a library of podcasts, CourseCasts, featuring a "CourseCast of the Week," and download them to your mp3 player at *http://coursecasts.course.com*.

Our fast-paced world is driven by technology. You know because you're an active participant—always on the go, always keeping up with technological trends, and always learning new ways to embrace technology to power your life.

Ken Baldauf, a faculty member of the Florida State University Computer Science Department, is responsible for teaching technology classes to thousands of FSU students each year. He knows what you know; he knows what you want to learn. He's also an expert in the latest technology and will sort through and aggregate the most pertinent news and information so you can spend your time enjoying technology, rather than trying to figure it out.

Visit us at *http://coursecasts.course.com* to learn on the go!

Brief Contents

Contents

POWERPOINT 2007   **Unit D: Finishing a Presentation**   **73**

Read This Before You Begin

Frequently Asked Questions

What are Data Files?

A Data File is a partially completed PowerPoint presentation or another type of file that you use to complete the steps in the units and exercises to create the final document that you submit to your instructor. Each unit opener page lists the Data Files that you need for that unit.

Where are the Data Files?

Your instructor will provide the Data Files to you or direct you to a location on a network drive from which you can download them. Alternatively, you can follow the instructions on the next page to download the Data Files from this book's Web page.

What software was used to write and test this book?

This book was written and tested using a typical installation of Microsoft Office 2007 on a computer with a typical installation of Windows Vista.

The browser used for any steps that require a browser is Internet Explorer 7. If you are using this book on Windows XP, please see the next page, Important Notes for Windows XP Users. If you are using this book on Windows Vista, please see the Appendix.

Do I need to be connected to the Internet to complete the steps and exercises in this book?

Some of the exercises in this book assume that your computer is connected to the Internet. If you are not connected to the Internet, see your instructor for information on how to complete the exercises.

What do I do if my screen is different from the figures shown in this book?

This book was written and tested on computers with monitors set at a resolution of 1024 × 768. If your screen shows more or less information than the figures in the book, your monitor is probably set at a higher or lower resolution. If you don't see something on your screen, you might have to scroll down or up to see the object identified in the figures.

The Ribbon (the blue area at the top of the screen) in Microsoft Office 2007 adapts to different resolutions. If your monitor is set at a lower resolution than 1024 × 768, you might not see all of the buttons shown in the figures. The groups of buttons will always appear, but the entire group might be condensed into a single button that you need to click to access the buttons described in the instructions. For example, the figures and steps in this book assume that the Editing group on the Home tab in Word looks like the following:

1024 × 768 Editing Group

Editing Group on the Home Tab of the Ribbon at 1024 × 768

If your resolution is set to 800 × 600, the Ribbon in Word will look like the following figure, and you will need to click the Editing button to access the buttons that are visible in the Editing group.

800 × 600 Editing Group

Editing Group on the Home Tab of the Ribbon at 800 × 600

800 × 600 Editing Group Clicked

Editing Group on the Home Tab of the Ribbon at 800 × 600 is selected to show available buttons

Important Notes for Windows XP Users

The screenshots in this book show Microsoft Office 2007 running on Windows Vista. However, if you are using Microsoft Windows XP, you can still use this book because Office 2007 runs virtually the same on both platforms. There are a few differences that you will encounter if you are using Windows XP. Read this section to understand the differences.

Dialog boxes

If you are a Windows XP user, dialog boxes shown in this book will look slightly different than what you see on your screen. Dialog boxes for Windows XP have a blue title bar, instead of a gray title bar. However, beyond this superficial difference in appearance, the options in the dialog boxes across platforms are the same. For instance, the screen shots below show the Font dialog box running on Windows XP and the Font dialog box running on Windows Vista.

FIGURE 1: Dialog box in Windows XP

FIGURE 2: Dialog box in Windows Vista

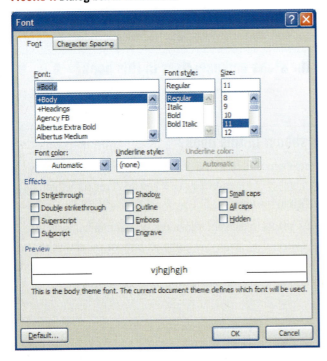

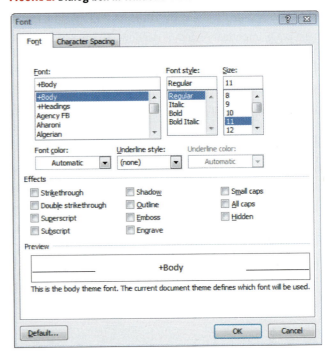

Alternate Steps for Windows XP Users

Nearly all of the steps in this book work exactly the same for Windows XP users. However, there are a few tasks that will require you to complete slightly different steps. This section provides alternate steps for a few specific skills.

Starting a program

1. Click the Start button on the taskbar
2. Point to All Programs, point to Microsoft Office, then click the application you want to use

FIGURE 3: Starting a program

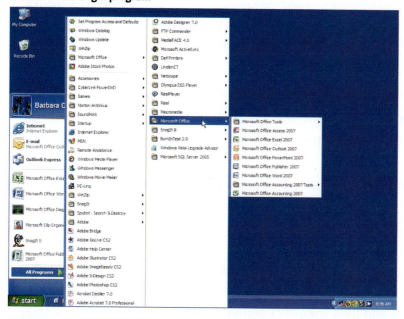

Saving a file for the first time

1. Click the Office button, then click Save As
2. Type a name for your file in the File Name text box
3. Click the Save in list arrow, then navigate to the drive and folder where you store your Data Files
4. Click Save

FIGURE 4: Save As dialog box

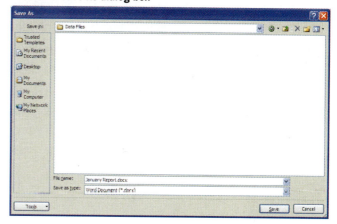

Opening a file

1. Click the Office button, then click Open
2. Click the Look in list arrow, then navigate to the drive and folder where you store your Data Files
3. Click the file you want to open
4. Click Open

Figure 5: Open dialog box

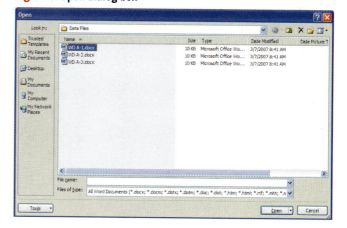

Downloading Data Files for This Book

In order to complete many of the lesson steps and exercises in this book, you are asked to open and save Data Files. A **Data File** is a partially completed PowerPoint presentation or another type of file that you use as a starting point to complete the steps in the units and exercises. The benefit of using a Data File is that it saves you the time and effort needed to create a file; you can simply open a Data File, save it with a new name (so the original file remains intact), then make changes to it to complete lesson steps or an exercise. Your instructor will provide the Data Files to you or direct you to a location on a network drive from which you can download them. Alternatively, you can follow the instructions in this lesson to download the Data Files from this book's Web page.

1. Start Internet Explorer, type www.course.com in the address bar, then press [Enter]

2. When the Course.com Web site opens, click the Student Downloads link

3. On the Student Downloads page, click in the Search text box, type 9781423905233, then click Go

QUICK TIP

You can also click Student Downloads on the right side of the product page.

4. When the page opens for this textbook, in the left navigation bar, click the Download Student Files link, then, on the Student Downloads page, click the Data Files link

5. If the File Download – Security Warning dialog box opens, click Save. (If no dialog box appears, skip this step and go to Step 6)

TROUBLE

If a dialog box opens telling you that the download is complete, click Close.

6. If the Save As dialog box opens, click the Save in list arrow at the top of the dialog box, select a folder on your USB drive or hard disk to download the file to, then click Save

7. Close Internet Explorer and then open My Computer or Windows Explorer and display the contents of the drive and folder to which you downloaded the file

8. Double-click the file 905233.exe in the drive or folder, then, if the Open File – Security Warning dialog box opens, click Run

QUICK TIP

By default, the files will extract to C:\CourseTechnology\905233

9. In the WinZip Self-Extractor window, navigate to the drive and folder where you want to unzip the files to, then click Unzip

10. When the WinZip Self-Extractor displays a dialog box listing the number of files that have unzipped successfully, click OK , click Close in the WinZip Self-Extractor dialog box, then close Windows Explorer or My Computer

You are now ready to open the required files.

Getting Started with Microsoft Office 2007

Files You Will Need:

OFFICE A-1.xlsx

Microsoft Office 2007 is a group of software programs designed to help you create documents, collaborate with co-workers, and track and analyze information. Each program is designed so you can work quickly and efficiently to create professional-looking results. You use different Office programs to accomplish specific tasks, such as writing a letter or producing a sales presentation, yet all the programs have a similar look and feel. Once you become familiar with one program, you'll find it easy to transfer your knowledge to the others. This unit introduces you to the most frequently used programs in Office, as well as common features they all share.

OBJECTIVES

Understand the Office 2007 Suite

Start and exit an Office program

View the Office 2007 user interface

Create and save a file

Open a file and save it with a new name

View and print your work

Get Help and close a file

Understanding the Office 2007 Suite

Microsoft Office 2007 features an intuitive, context-sensitive user interface, so you can get up to speed faster and use advanced features with greater ease. The programs in Office are bundled together in a group called a **suite** (although you can also purchase them separately). The Office suite is available in several configurations, but all include Word and Excel. Other configurations include PowerPoint, Access, Outlook, Publisher, and/or others.  Each program in Office is best suited for completing specific types of tasks, though there is some overlap in terms of their capabilities.

DETAILS

The Office programs covered in this book include:

• **Microsoft Office Word 2007**

When you need to create any kind of text-based document, such as memos, newsletters, or multi-page reports, Word is the program to use. You can easily make your documents look great by inserting eye-catching graphics and using formatting tools such as themes. **Themes** are predesigned combinations of color and formatting attributes you can apply, and are available in most Office programs. The Word document shown in Figure A-1 was formatted with the Solstice theme.

• **Microsoft Office Excel 2007**

Excel is the perfect solution when you need to work with numeric values and make calculations. It puts the power of formulas, functions, charts, and other analytical tools into the hands of every user, so you can analyze sales projections, figure out loan payments, and present your findings in style. The Excel worksheet shown in Figure A-1 tracks personal expenses. Because Excel automatically recalculates results whenever a value changes, the information is always up-to-date. A chart illustrates how the monthly expenses are broken down.

• **Microsoft Office PowerPoint 2007**

Using PowerPoint, it's easy to create powerful presentations complete with graphics, transitions, and even a soundtrack. Using professionally designed themes and clip art, you can quickly and easily create dynamic slideshows such as the one shown in Figure A-1.

• **Microsoft Office Access 2007**

Access helps you keep track of large amounts of quantitative data, such as product inventories or employee records. The form shown in Figure A-1 was created for a grocery store inventory database. Employees use the form to enter data about each item. Using Access enables employees to quickly find specific information such as price and quantity, without hunting through store shelves and stockrooms.

Microsoft Office has benefits beyond the power of each program, including:

• **Common user interface: Improving business processes**

Because the Office suite programs have a similar **interface**, or look and feel, your experience using one program's tools makes it easy to learn those in the other programs. Office documents are **compatible** with one another, meaning that you can easily incorporate, or **integrate**, an Excel chart into a PowerPoint slide, or an Access table into a Word document.

• **Collaboration: Simplifying how people work together**

Office recognizes the way people do business today, and supports the emphasis on communication and knowledge-sharing within companies and across the globe. All Office programs include the capability to incorporate feedback—called **online collaboration**—across the Internet or a company network.

FIGURE A-1: Microsoft Office 2007 documents

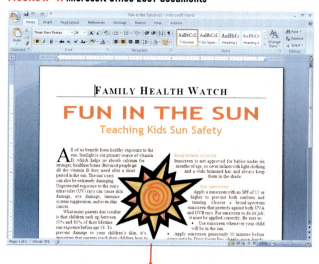

Word document

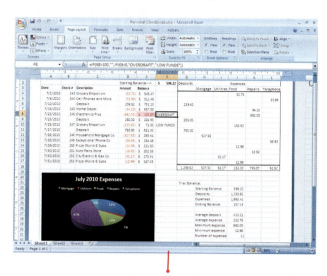

Excel worksheet

PowerPoint presentation

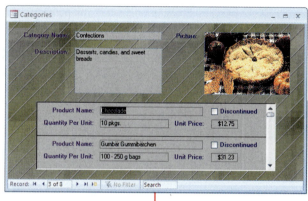

Access database form

Deciding which program to use

Every Office program includes tools that go far beyond what you might expect. For example, although Excel is primarily designed for making calculations, you can use it to create a database. So when you're planning a project, how do you decide which Office program to use? The general rule of thumb is to use the program best suited for your intended task, and make use of supporting tools in the program if you need them. Word is best for creating text-based documents, Excel is best for making mathematical calculations, PowerPoint is best for preparing presentations, and Access is best for managing quantitative data. Although the capabilities of Office are so vast that you *could* create an inventory in Excel or a budget in Word, you'll find greater flexibility and efficiency by using the program designed for the task. And remember, you can always create a file in one program, and then insert it in a document in another program when you need to, such as including sales projections (Excel) in a memo (Word).

Starting and Exiting an Office Program

The first step in using an Office program is of course to open, or **launch**, it on your computer. You have a few choices for how to launch a program, but the easiest way is to click the Start button on the Windows taskbar, or to double-click an icon on your desktop. You can have multiple programs open on your computer simultaneously, and you can move between open programs by clicking the desired program or document button on the taskbar or by using the [Alt][Tab] keyboard shortcut combination. When working, you'll often want to open multiple programs in Office, and switch among them throughout the day. Begin by launching a few Office programs now.

STEPS

QUICK TIP

You can also launch a program by double-clicking a desktop icon or clicking an entry on the Recent Items menu.

1. **Click the Start button 🏁 on the taskbar**

   The Start menu opens, as shown in Figure A-2. If the taskbar is hidden, you can display it by pointing to the bottom of the screen. Depending on your taskbar property settings, the taskbar may be displayed at all times, or only when you point to that area of the screen. For more information, or to change your taskbar properties, consult your instructor or technical support person.

2. **Point to All Programs, click Microsoft Office, then click Microsoft Office Word 2007**

   Microsoft Office Word 2007 starts and the program window opens on your screen.

QUICK TIP

It is not necessary to close one program before opening another.

3. **Click 🏁 on the taskbar, point to All Programs, click Microsoft Office, then click Microsoft Office Excel 2007**

   Microsoft Office Excel 2007 starts and the program window opens, as shown in Figure A-3. Word is no longer visible, but it remains open. The taskbar displays a button for each open program and document. Because this Excel document is **active**, or in front and available, the Microsoft Excel – Book1 button on the taskbar appears in a darker shade.

4. **Click Document1 – Microsoft Word on the taskbar**

   Clicking a button on the taskbar activates that program and document. The Word program window is now in front, and the Document1 – Microsoft Word taskbar button appears shaded.

QUICK TIP

If there isn't room on your taskbar to display the entire name of each button, you can point to any button to see the full name in a Screentip.

5. **Click 🏁 on the taskbar, point to All Programs, click Microsoft Office, then click Microsoft Office PowerPoint 2007**

   Microsoft Office PowerPoint 2007 starts, and becomes the active program.

6. **Click Microsoft Excel – Book1 on the taskbar**

   Excel is now the active program.

QUICK TIP

As you work in Windows, your computer adapts to your activities. You may notice that after clicking the Start button, the name of the program you want to open appears in the Start menu; if so, you can click it to start the program.

7. **Click 🏁 on the taskbar, point to All Programs, click Microsoft Office, then click Microsoft Office Access 2007**

   Microsoft Office Access 2007 starts, and becomes the active program.

8. **Point to the taskbar to display it, if necessary**

   Four Office programs are open simultaneously.

9. **Click the Office button 🏁, then click Exit Access, as shown in Figure A-4**

   Access closes, leaving Excel active and Word and PowerPoint open.

FIGURE A-2: Start menu

FIGURE A-3: Excel program window and Windows taskbar

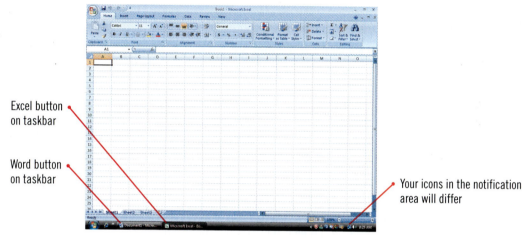

Excel button
on taskbar

Word button
on taskbar

Your icons in the notification
area will differ

FIGURE A-4: Exiting Microsoft Office Access

Microsoft
Office button

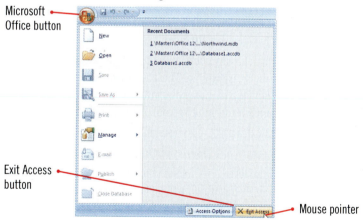

Exit Access
button

Mouse pointer

Using shortcut keys to move between Office programs

As an alternative to the Windows taskbar, you can use a keyboard shortcut to move among open Office programs. The [Alt][Tab] keyboard combination lets you either switch quickly to the next open program, or choose one from a palette. To switch immediately to the next open program, press [Alt][Tab]. To choose from all open programs, press and hold [Alt], then press and release [Tab] without releasing [Alt]. A palette opens on screen, displaying the icon and filename of each open program and file. Each time you press [Tab] while holding [Alt], the selection cycles to the next open file. Release [Alt] when the program/file you want to activate is selected.

Viewing the Office 2007 User Interface

One of the benefits of using Office is that the programs have much in common, making them easy to learn and making it simple to move from one to another. Individual Office programs have always shared many features, but the innovations in the Office 2007 user interface mean even greater similarity among them all. That means you can also use your knowledge of one program to get up to speed in another. A **user interface** is a collective term for all the ways you interact with a software program. The user interface in Office 2007 includes a more intuitive way of choosing commands, working with files, and navigating in the program window. Familiarize yourself with some of the common interface elements in Office by examining the PowerPoint program window.

STEPS

1. **Click Microsoft PowerPoint – [Presentation1] on the taskbar**

   PowerPoint becomes the active program. Refer to Figure A-5 to identify common elements of the Office user interface. The **document window** occupies most of the screen. In PowerPoint, a blank slide appears in the document window, so you can build your slide show. At the top of every Office program window is a **title bar**, which displays the document and program name. Below the title bar is the **Ribbon**, which displays commands you're likely to need for the current task. Commands are organized into **tabs**. The tab names appear at the top of the Ribbon, and the active tab appears in front with its name highlighted. The Ribbon in every Office program includes tabs specific to the program, but all include a Home tab on the far left, for the most popular tasks in that program.

2. **Click the Office button**

   The Office menu opens. This menu contains commands common to most Office programs, such as opening a file, saving a file, and closing the current program. Next to the Office button is the **Quick Access toolbar**, which includes buttons for common Office commands.

3. **Click again to close it, then point to the Save button on the Quick Access toolbar, *but do not click it***

   You can point to any button in Office to see a description; this is a good way to learn the available choices.

4. **Click the Design tab on the Ribbon**

   To display a different tab, you click its name on the Ribbon. Each tab arranges related commands into **groups** to make features easy to find. The Themes group displays available themes in a **gallery**, or palette of choices you can browse. Many groups contain a **dialog box launcher**, an icon you can click to open a dialog box or task pane for the current group, which offers an alternative way to choose commands.

5. **Move the mouse pointer over the Aspect theme in the Themes group as shown in Figure A-6, *but do not click the mouse button***

   Because you have not clicked the theme, you have not actually made any changes to the slide. With the **Live Preview** feature, you can point to a choice, see the results right in the document, and then decide whether you want to make the change.

6. **Move away from the Ribbon and towards the slide**

   If you clicked the Aspect theme, it would be applied to this slide. Instead, the slide remains unchanged.

7. **Point to the Zoom slider on the status bar, then drag to the right until the Zoom percentage reads 166%**

   The slide display is enlarged. Zoom tools are located on the status bar. You can drag the slider or click the plus and minus buttons to zoom in/out on an area of interest. The percentage tells you the zoom effect.

8. **Drag the Zoom slider on the status bar to the left until the Zoom percentage reads 73%**

FIGURE A-5: PowerPoint program window

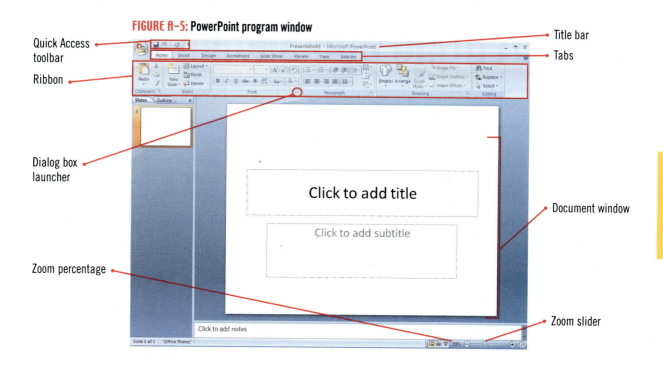

Quick Access toolbar

Ribbon

Dialog box launcher

Zoom percentage

Title bar

Tabs

Document window

Zoom slider

FIGURE A-6: Viewing a theme with Live Preview

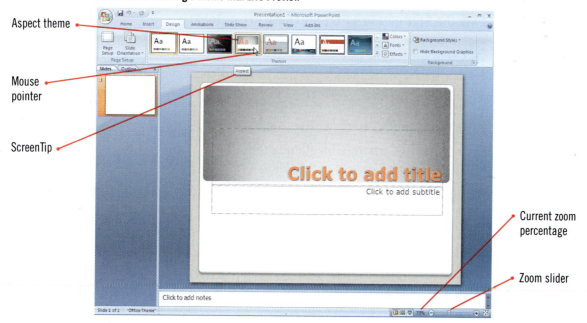

Aspect theme

Mouse pointer

ScreenTip

Current zoom percentage

Zoom slider

Customizing the Quick Access toolbar

You can customize the Quick Access toolbar to display your favorite commands. To do so, click the Customize Quick Access Toolbar button ⟱ in the title bar, then click the command you want to add. If you don't see the command in the list, click More Commands to open the Customize tab of the Options dialog box. In the Options dialog box, use the Choose commands from list to choose a category, click the desired command in the list on the left, click Add to add it to the Quick Access toolbar, then click OK. To remove a button from the toolbar, click the name in the list on the right, then click Remove. To add a command to the Quick Access toolbar on the fly, simply right-click the button on the Ribbon, then click Add to Quick Access Toolbar on the shortcut menu. You can also use the Customize Quick Access Toolbar button to move the toolbar below the ribbon, by clicking Show Below the Ribbon, or to minimize the Ribbon so it takes up less space onscreen. If you click Minimize the Ribbon, the Ribbon is minimized to display only the tabs. When you click a tab, the Ribbon opens so you can choose a command; once you choose a command, the Ribbon closes again, and only the tabs are visible.

Creating and Saving a File

When working in a program, one of the first things you need to do is to create and save a file. A **file** is a stored collection of data. Saving a file enables you to work on a project now, then put it away and work on it again later. In some Office programs, including Word, Excel, and PowerPoint, a new file is automatically created when you start the program, so all you have to do is enter some data and save it. In Access, you must expressly create a file before you enter any data. You should give your files meaningful names and save them in an appropriate location, so they're easy to find. Use Microsoft Word to familiarize yourself with the process of creating and saving a document. First you'll type some notes about a possible location for a corporate meeting, then you'll save the information for later use.

STEPS

1. **Click Document1 – Microsoft Word on the taskbar**

2. **Type Locations for Corporate Meeting, then press [Enter] twice**

   The text appears in the document window, and a cursor blinks on a new blank line. The cursor indicates where the next typed text will appear.

3. **Type Las Vegas, NV, press [Enter], type Orlando, FL, press [Enter], type Chicago, IL, press [Enter] twice, then type your name**

   Compare your document to Figure A-7.

   QUICK TIP

   A filename can be up to 255 characters, including a file extension, and can include upper- or lowercase characters and spaces, but not ?, ", /, \, <, >, *, |, or :.

4. ▶ **Click the Save button 🖫 on the Quick Access toolbar**

   Because this is the first time you are saving this document, the Save As dialog box opens, as shown in Figure A-8. The Save As dialog box includes options for assigning a filename and storage location. Once you save a file for the first time, clicking 🖫 saves any changes to the file *without* opening the Save As dialog box, because no additional information is needed. In the Address bar, Office displays the default location for where to save the file, but you can change to any location. In the File name field, Office displays a suggested name for the document based on text in the file, but you can enter a different name.

5. **Type Potential Corporate Meeting Locations**

   The text you type replaces the highlighted text.

   QUICK TIP

   You can create a desktop icon that you can double-click to both launch a program and open a document, by saving it to the desktop.

6. ▶ **In the Save As dialog box, use the Address bar or Navigation pane to navigate to the drive and folder where you store your Data Files**

   Many students store files on a flash drive or Zip drive, but you can also store files on your computer, a network drive, or any storage device indicated by your instructor or technical support person.

   QUICK TIP

   To create a new blank file when a file is open, click the Office button, click New, then click Create.

7. ▶ **Click Save**

   The Save As dialog box closes, the new file is saved to the location you specified, then the name of the document appears in the title bar, as shown in Figure A-9. (You may or may not see a file extension.) See Table A-1 for a description of the different types of files you create in Office, and the file extensions associated with each. You can save a file in an earlier version of a program by choosing from the list of choices in the Save as type list arrow in the Save As dialog box.

TABLE A-1: Common filenames and default file extensions

File created in	is called a	and has the default extension
Excel	workbook	.xlsx
Word	document	.docx
Access	database	.accdb
PowerPoint	presentation	.pptx

FIGURE A-7: Creating a document in Word

Save button

Your name should appear here

Insertion point

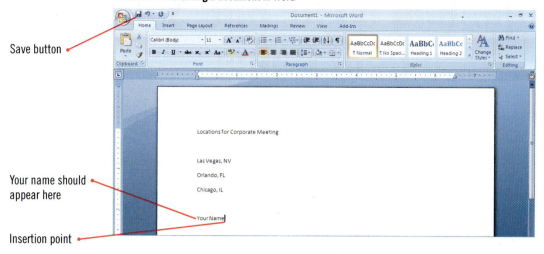

FIGURE A-8: Save As dialog box

Address bar

Navigation pane; your links and Folders setting may differ

File name field; your computer may not be set to display file extensions

Previous Locations list arrow

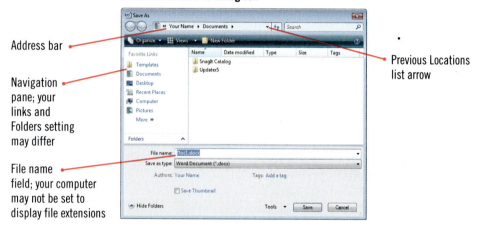

FIGURE A-9: Named Word document

Name appears in title bar

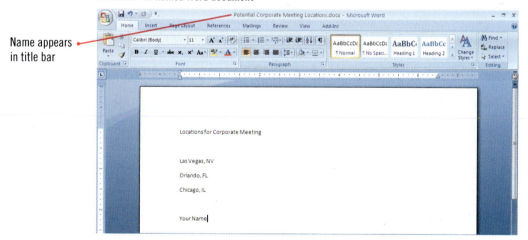

Using the Office Clipboard

You can use the Office Clipboard to cut and copy items from one Office program and paste them into others. The Clipboard can store a maximum of 24 items. To access it, open the Office Clipboard task pane by clicking the launcher in the Clipboard group in the Home tab. Each time you copy a selection, it is saved in the Office Clipboard. Each entry in the Office Clipboard includes an icon that tells you the program in which it was created. To paste an entry, click in the document where you want it to appear, then click the item in the Office Clipboard. To delete an item from the Office Clipboard, right-click the item, then click Delete.

Opening a File and Saving it with a New Name

In many cases as you work in Office, you start with a blank document, but often you need to use an existing file. It might be a file you or a co-worker created earlier as a work-in-progress, or it could be a complete document that you want to use as the basis for another. For example, you might want to create a budget for this year using the budget you created last year; you could type in all the categories and information from scratch, or you could open last year's budget, save it with a new name, and just make changes to update it for the current year. By opening the existing file and saving it with the Save As command, you create a duplicate that you can modify to your heart's content, while the original file remains intact. Use Excel to open an existing workbook file, and save it with a new name so the original remains unchanged.

STEPS

1. **Click Microsoft Excel – Book1 on the taskbar, click the Office button 🏢, then click Open**
   The Open dialog box opens, where you can navigate to any drive or folder location accessible to your computer to locate a file.

2. **In the Open dialog box, navigate to the drive and folder where you store your Data Files**
   The files available in the current folder are listed, as shown in Figure A-10. This folder contains one file.

3. **Click OFFICE A-1.xlsx, then click Open**
   The dialog box closes and the file opens in Excel. An Excel file is an electronic spreadsheet, so it looks different from a Word document or a PowerPoint slide.

4. **Click 🏢, then click Save As**
   The Save As dialog box opens, and the current filename is highlighted in the File name text box. Using the Save As command enables you to create a copy of the current, existing file with a new name. This action preserves the original file, and creates a new file that you can modify.

5. **Navigate to the drive and folder where your Data Files are stored if necessary, type Budget for Corporate Meeting in the File name text box, as shown in Figure A-11, then click Save**
   A copy of the existing document is created with the new name. The original file, Office A-1.xlsx, closes automatically.

6. **Click cell A19, type your name, then press [Enter], as shown in Figure A-12**
   In Excel, you enter data in cells, which are formed by the intersection of a row and a column. Cell A19 is at the intersection of column A and row 19. When you press [Enter], the cell pointer moves to cell A20.

7. **Click the Save button 🖫 on the Quick Access toolbar**
   Your name appears in the worksheet, and your changes to the file are saved.

Exploring File Open options

You might have noticed that the Open button on the Open dialog box includes an arrow. In a dialog box, if a button includes an arrow you can click the button to invoke the command, or you can click the arrow to choose from a list of related commands. The Open button list arrow includes several related commands, including Open Read-Only and Open as Copy. Clicking Open Read-Only opens a file that you can only save by saving it with a new name; you cannot save changes to the original file. Clicking Open as Copy creates a copy of the file already saved and named with the word "Copy" in the title. Like the Save As command, these commands provide additional ways to use copies of existing files while ensuring that original files do not get inadvertently changed.

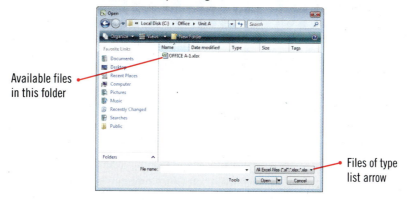

Available files in this folder

Files of type list arrow

FIGURE A-11: Save As dialog box

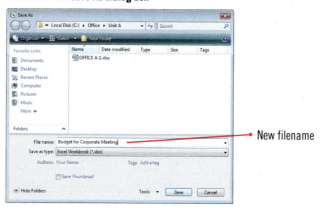

New filename

FIGURE A-12: Adding your name to the worksheet

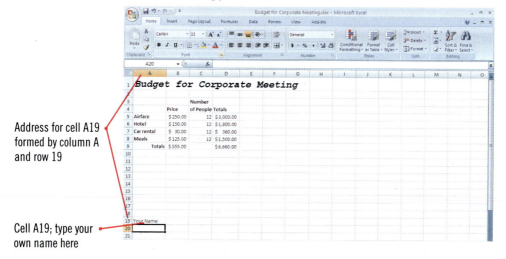

Address for cell A19 formed by column A and row 19

Cell A19; type your own name here

Working in Compatibility mode

Not everyone upgrades to the newest version of Office. As a general rule, new software versions are **backward-compatible**, meaning that documents saved by an older version can be read by newer software. The reverse is not always true, so Office 2007 includes a feature called Compatibility mode. When you open a file created in an earlier version of Office, "Compatibility Mode" appears in the title bar, letting you know the file was created in an earlier, but usable version of the program. If you are working with someone who may not be using the newest version of the software, you can avoid possible incompatibility problems by saving your file in another, earlier format. To do this, click the Office button, point to the Save As command, then click a choice on the Save As submenu. For example, if you're working in Excel, click Excel 97-2003 Workbook format. When the Save As dialog box opens, you'll notice that the Save as type box reads "Excel 97-2003 Workbook" instead of the default "Excel Workbook." To see more file format choices, such as Excel 97-2003 Template or Microsoft Excel 5.0/95 Workbook, click Other Formats on the Save As submenu. In the Save As dialog box, click the Save as type button, click the choice you think matches what your co-worker is using, then click Save.

Viewing and Printing Your Work

If your computer is connected to a printer or a print server, you can easily print any Office document. Printing can be as simple as clicking a button, or as involved as customizing the print job by printing only selected pages or making other choices, and/or **previewing** the document to see exactly what a document will look like when it is printed. (In order for printing and previewing to work, a printer must be installed.) In addition to using Print Preview, each Microsoft Office program lets you switch among various **views** of the document window, to show more or fewer details or a different combination of elements that make it easier to complete certain tasks, such as formatting or reading text. You can also increase or decrease your view of a document, so you can see more or less of it on the screen at once. Changing your view of a document does not affect the file in any way, it affects only the way it looks on screen. Experiment with changing your view of a Word document, and then preview and print your work.

STEPS

1. **Click Potential Corporate Meeting Locations – Microsoft Word on the taskbar**

   Word becomes the active program, and the document fills the screen.

2. **Click the View tab on the Ribbon**

   In most Office programs, the View tab on the Ribbon includes groups and commands for changing your view of the current document. You can also change views using the View buttons on the status bar.

3. **Click Web Layout button in the Document Views group on the View tab**

   The view changes to Web Layout view, as shown in Figure A-13. This view shows how the document will look if you save it as a Web page.

> **QUICK TIP**
>
> You can also use the Zoom button in the Zoom group of the View tab to enlarge or reduce a document's appearance.

4. **Click the Zoom in button ⊕ on the status bar eight times until the zoom percentage reads 180%**

   Zooming in, or choosing a higher percentage, makes a document appear bigger on screen, but less of it fits on the screen at once; **zooming out**, or choosing a lower percentage, lets you see more of the document but at a reduced size.

5. **Drag the Zoom slider ▽ on the status bar to the center mark**

   The Zoom slider lets you zoom in and out without opening a dialog box or clicking buttons.

6. **Click the Print Layout button on the View tab**

   You return to Print Layout view, the default view in Microsoft Word.

7. **Click the Office button 🔘, point to Print, then click Print Preview**

   The Print Preview presents the most accurate view of how your document will look when printed, displaying the entire page on screen at once. Compare your screen to Figure A-14. The Ribbon in Print Preview contains a single tab, also known as a **program** tab, with commands specific to Print Preview. The commands on this tab facilitate viewing and changing overall settings such as margins and page size.

> **QUICK TIP**
>
> You can open the Print dialog box from any view by clicking the Office button, then clicking Print.

8. **Click the Print button on the Ribbon**

   The Print dialog box opens, as shown in Figure A-15. You can use this dialog box to change which pages to print, the number of printed copies, and even the number of pages you print on each page. If you have multiple printers from which to choose, you can change from one installed printer by clicking the Name list arrow, then clicking the name of the installed printer you want to use.

9. **Click OK, then click the Close Print Preview button on the Ribbon**

   A copy of the document prints, and Print Preview closes.

FIGURE A-13: Web Layout view

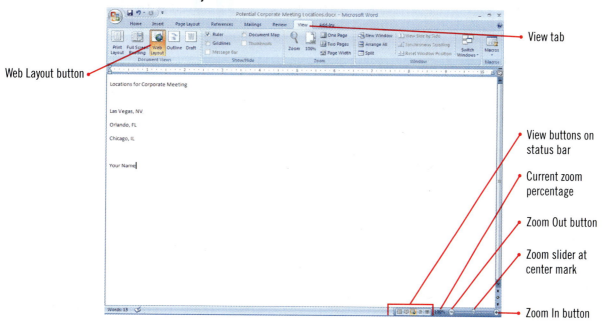

Web Layout button

View tab

View buttons on status bar

Current zoom percentage

Zoom Out button

Zoom slider at center mark

Zoom In button

FIGURE A-14: Print Preview screen

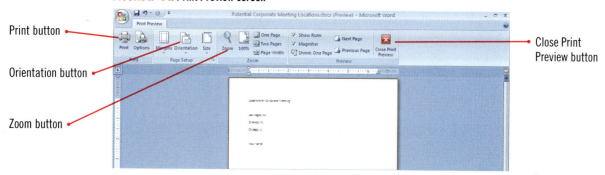

Print button

Orientation button

Zoom button

Close Print Preview button

FIGURE A-15: Print dialog box

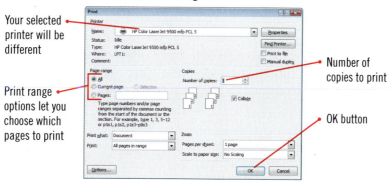

Your selected printer will be different

Print range options let you choose which pages to print

Number of copies to print

OK button

Using the Print Screen feature to create a screen capture

At some point you may want to create a screen capture. A **screen capture** is a snapshot of your screen, as if you took a picture of it with a camera. You might want to take a screen capture if an error message occurs and you want Technical Support to see exactly what's on the screen. Or perhaps your instructor wants to see what your screen looks like when you create a particular document. To create a screen capture, press [PrtScn]. (Keyboards differ, but you may find the [PrtScn] button on the Insert key in or near your keyboard's function keys. You may have to press the [F Lock] key to enable the Function keys.) Pressing this key places a digital image of your screen in the Windows temporary storage area known as the **Clipboard**. Open the document where you want the screen capture to appear, click the Home tab on the Ribbon (if necessary), then click Paste on the Home tab. The screen capture is pasted into the document.

Getting Help and Closing a File

You can get comprehensive help at any time by pressing [F1] in an Office program. You can also get help in the form of a ScreenTip by pointing to almost any icon in the program window. When you're finished working in an Office document, you have a few choices regarding ending your work session. You can close a file or exit a program by using the Office button or by clicking a button on the title bar. Closing a file leaves a program running, while exiting a program closes all the open files in that program as well as the program itself. In all cases, Office reminds you if you try to close a file or exit a program and your document contains unsaved changes. Explore the Help system in Microsoft Office, and then close your documents and exit any open programs.

STEPS

1. **Point to the Zoom button on the View tab of the Ribbon**
   A ScreenTip appears that describes how the Zoom button works.

2. **Press [F1]**
   The Word Help window opens, as shown in Figure A-16, displaying the home page for help in Word. Each entry is a hyperlink you can click to open a list of related topics. This window also includes a toolbar of useful Help commands and a Search field. The connection status at the bottom of the Help window indicates that the connection to Office Online is active. Office Online supplements the help content available on your computer with a wide variety of up-to-date topics, templates, and training.

   > **QUICK TIP**
   > If you are not connected to the Internet, the Help window displays only the help content available on your computer.

3. **Click the Getting help link in the Table of Contents pane**
   The icon next to Getting help changes and its list of subtopics expands.

4. **Click the Work with the Help window link in the topics list in the left pane**
   The topic opens in the right pane, as shown in Figure A-17.

   > **QUICK TIP**
   > You can also open the Help window by clicking the Microsoft Office Help button ❷ to the right of the tabs on the Ribbon.

5. **Click the Hide Table of Contents button 📖 on the Help toolbar**
   The left pane closes, as shown in Figure A-18.

6. **Click the Show Table of Contents button 📖 on the Help toolbar, scroll to the bottom of the left pane, click the Accessibility link in the Table of Contents pane, click the Use the keyboard to work with Ribbon programs link, read the information in the right pane, then click the Help window Close button**

   > **QUICK TIP**
   > You can print the current topic by clicking the Print button 🖨 on the Help toolbar to open the Print dialog box.

7. **Click the Office button 🔵, then click Close; if a dialog box opens asking whether you want to save your changes, click Yes**
   The Potential Corporate Meeting Locations document closes, leaving the Word program open.

8. **Click 🔵, then click Exit Word**
   Microsoft Office Word closes, and the Excel program window is active.

9. **Click 🔵, click Exit Excel, click the PowerPoint button on the taskbar if necessary, click 🔵, then click Exit PowerPoint**
   Microsoft Office Excel and Microsoft Office PowerPoint both close.

FIGURE A-16: Word Help window

Help toolbar

Search field

Hide Table of
Contents
button

The colors
of your links
may differ

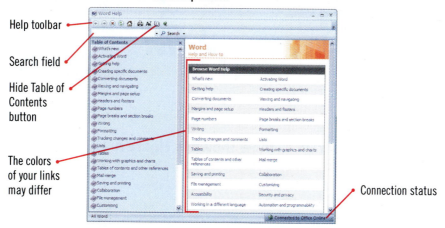

Connection status

FIGURE A-17: Work with the Help window

Print button

Icon indicates
expanded topic

Work with
the Help
window link

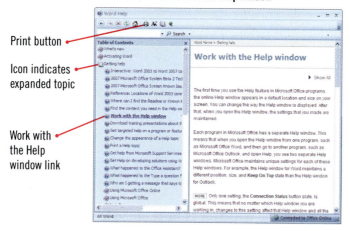

FIGURE A-18: Help window with Table of Contents closed

Show Table of
Contents button

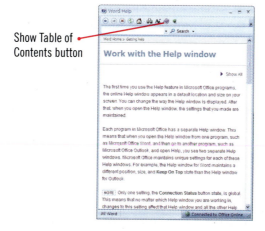

Recovering a document

Sometimes while you are using Office, you may experience a power failure or your computer may "freeze," making it impossible to continue working. If this type of interruption occurs, each Office program has a built-in recovery feature that allows you to open and save files that were open at the time of the interruption. When you restart the program(s) after an interruption, the Document Recovery task pane opens on the left side of your screen displaying both original and recovered versions of the files that were open. If you're not sure which file to open (original or recovered), it's usually better to open the recovered file because it will contain the latest information. You can, however, open and review all versions of the file that were recovered and save the best one. Each file listed in the Document Recovery task pane displays a list arrow with options that allow you to open the file, save it as is, delete it, or show repairs made to it during recovery.

Practice

▼ CONCEPTS REVIEW

Label the elements of the program window shown in Figure A-19.

FIGURE A-19

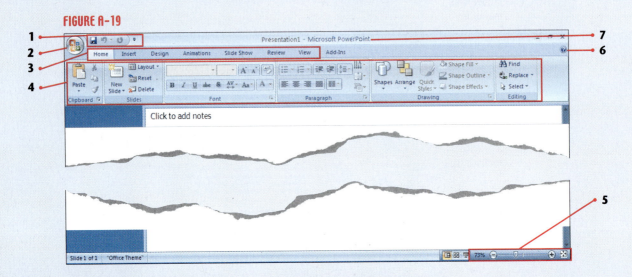

Match each project with the program for which it is best suited.

8. Microsoft Office PowerPoint
9. Microsoft Office Excel
10. Microsoft Office Word
11. Microsoft Office Access

a. Corporate expansion budget with expense projections
b. Business résumé for a job application
c. Auto parts store inventory
d. Presentation for Board of Directors meeting

▼ INDEPENDENT CHALLENGE 1

You just accepted an administrative position with a local car dealership that's recently invested in computers and is now considering purchasing Microsoft Office. You are asked to propose ways Office might help the dealership. You produce your proposal in Microsoft Word.

a. Start Word, then save the document as **Microsoft Office Proposal** in the drive and folder where you store your Data Files.

b. Type **Microsoft Office Word**, press [Enter] twice, type **Microsoft Office Excel**, press [Enter] twice, type **Microsoft Office PowerPoint**, press [Enter] twice, type **Microsoft Office Access**, press [Enter] twice, then type your name.

c. Click the line beneath each program name, type at least two tasks suited to that program, then press [Enter].

d. Save your work, then print one copy of this document.

Advanced Challenge Exercise

■ Press the [PrtScn] button to create a screen capture, then press [Ctrl][V].
■ Save and print the document.

e. Exit Word.

Creating a Presentation in PowerPoint 2007

Files You Will Need:

No files needed.

Microsoft Office PowerPoint 2007 is a powerful computer software program that enables you to create visually dynamic presentations. With PowerPoint, you can create individual slides and display them as a slide show on your computer, a video projector, or over the Internet. Ellen Latsky is the European tour developer for Quest Specialty Travel (QST), an adventure tour company committed to providing travel experiences that immerse travelers into world cultures. One of Ellen's responsibilities is to present new tour ideas for the upcoming travel season at the annual sales meeting held at the company's corporate offices. As a newly hired summer intern, Ellen has asked you to get acquainted with PowerPoint and then start work on the new tour ideas presentation.

OBJECTIVES

Define presentation software

Plan an effective presentation

Examine the PowerPoint window

Enter slide text

Add a new slide

Apply a design theme

Compare presentation views

Print a PowerPoint presentation

Defining Presentation Software

Presentation software is a computer program you use to organize and present information to others. Whether you are explaining a new product or moderating a meeting, presentation software can help you effectively communicate your ideas. You can use PowerPoint to create presentations, as well as speaker notes for the presenter and handouts for the audience. Table A-1 explains how your information can be presented using PowerPoint.  Ellen wants you to start work on the presentation that she will use to present the new European tour series. Because you are only somewhat familiar with PowerPoint, you get to work exploring its capabilities. Figure A-1 shows how a presentation looks printed as handouts. Figure A-2 shows how the same presentation might look printed as notes pages for a speaker.

DETAILS

You can easily complete the following tasks using PowerPoint:

- **Enter and edit text easily**

  Text editing and formatting commands in PowerPoint are organized by the task you are performing at the time, so you can enter, edit, and format text information simply and efficiently to produce the best results in the least amount of time.

- **Change the appearance of information**

  PowerPoint has many effects that can transform the way text, graphics, and slides appear. By exploring some of these capabilities, you discover how easy it is to change the appearance of your presentation.

- **Organize and arrange information**

  Once you start using PowerPoint, you won't have to spend much time making sure your information is correct and in the right order. With PowerPoint, you can quickly and easily rearrange and modify text, graphics, and slides in your presentation.

- **Incorporate information from other sources**

  Often, when you create presentations, you use information from a variety of sources. With PowerPoint, you can import text, photographs, numerical data, and facts from files created in such programs as Microsoft Word, Corel WordPerfect, Adobe Photoshop, Microsoft Excel, and Microsoft Access. You can also import graphic images from a variety of sources such as the Internet, other computers, a digital camera, or other graphics programs.

- **Present information in a variety of ways**

  With PowerPoint, you can present information using a variety of methods. For example, you can print handout pages or an outline of your presentation for audience members. You can display your presentation as an electronic slide show using your computer, or if you are presenting to a large group, you can use a video projector and a large screen. If you want to reach an even wider audience, you can publish the presentation to the Internet so people anywhere in the world can use a browser to view your presentation.

- **Collaborate on a presentation with others**

  PowerPoint makes it easy to collaborate with colleagues and coworkers to create a presentation using the Internet. You can use your e-mail program to send a presentation as an attachment to a colleague for feedback. If you have a large number of people that need to collaborate on a presentation, you can set up a shared workspace on the Internet so everyone in your group has access to the presentation.

TABLE A-1: Presenting information using PowerPoint

method	description
On-screen presentations	Run a slide show from your computer or through a video projector to a large screen
Notes	Print a page with the image of a slide and notes about each slide for yourself or your audience
Audience handouts	Print handouts with one, two, three, four, six, or nine slides on a page
Online meetings	View or work on a presentation with your colleagues in real time
Outline pages	Print a text outline of your presentation to highlight the main points
Overheads	Print PowerPoint slides directly to transparencies using a standard printer

Planning an Effective Presentation

Before you create a presentation, you need to have a basic idea of the information you want to communicate. PowerPoint is a powerful and flexible program that gives you the ability to start a presentation simply by entering the text of your message. If you have a design or theme you want to use, you can start the presentation by working on the design. In most cases you'll probably enter the text of your presentation into PowerPoint first and then tailor the design to the message and audience. When preparing your presentation, you need to keep in mind not only to whom you are giving it, but also where you are giving it. It is important to know what equipment you will need, such as a sound system, computer, or projector. 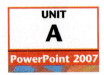 Use the planning guidelines below to help plan an effective presentation. Figure A-3 illustrates a storyboard for a well thought-out presentation.

DETAILS

In planning a presentation, it is important to:

- ### Determine and outline the message you want to communicate

    The more time you take developing the message and outline of your presentation, the better your presentation will be. A presentation with a clear message that reads like a story and is illustrated with visual aids will have the greatest impact on your audience. Start the presentation by describing the tour development goals, defining focus group data, and stating the tour strategy objectives. See Figure A-3.

- ### Verify the audience and the delivery location

    Audience and delivery location should be major factors in the type of presentation you create. For example, a presentation you develop for a staff meeting that is held in a conference room would not necessarily need to be as elaborate or detailed as a presentation that you develop for a large audience held in an auditorium. Room lighting, natural light, screen position, and room layout all affect how the audience responds to your presentation. This presentation will be delivered in a small auditorium to QST's management and sales team.

- ### Determine the type of output

    Output choices for a presentation include black-and-white or color handouts, on-screen slide show, or an online meeting. Consider the time demands and computer equipment availability as you decide which output types to produce. Because you are speaking in a small auditorium to a large group and have access to a computer and projection equipment, you decide that an on-screen slide show is the best output choice for your presentation.

- ### Determine the design

    Visual appeal, graphics, and design work to communicate your message. You can choose one of the professionally designed themes that come with PowerPoint, modify one of these themes, or create one of your own. You decide to choose one of PowerPoint's design themes to convey the new tour information.

- ### Decide what additional materials will be useful in the presentation

    You need to prepare not only the slides themselves but also supplementary materials, including speaker notes and handouts for the audience. You use speaker notes to help remember key details, and you pass out handouts for the audience to use as a reference during the presentation.

FIGURE A-3: Storyboard of the presentation

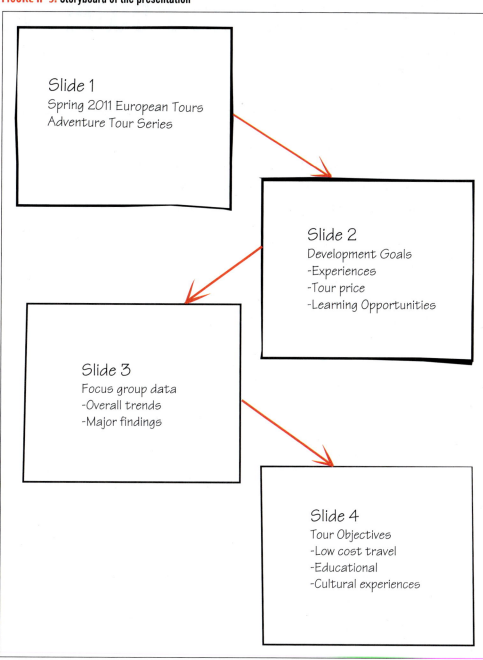

Understanding copyright

Intellectual property is any idea or creation of the human mind. Copyright law is a type of intellectual property law that protects works of authorship, including books, Web pages, computer games, music, artwork, and photographs. Copyright protects the expression of an idea, but not the underlying facts or concepts. In other words, the general subject matter is not protected, but how you express it is, such as when several people photograph the same sunset. Copyright attaches to any original work of authorship *as soon* as it is created, you *do not* have to register it with the Copyright Office or display the copyright symbol, ©.

Fair use is an exception to copyright and permits the public to use copyrighted material for certain purposes without obtaining prior consent from the owner. Determining whether fair use applies to a work depends on its purpose, the nature of the work, how much of the work you want to copy, and the effect on the work's value. Unauthorized use of protected work (such as downloading a photo or a song from the Web) is known as copyright infringement, and can lead to legal action.

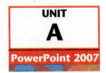

Examining the PowerPoint Window

When you first start PowerPoint, a blank slide appears in the PowerPoint window. PowerPoint has different **views** that allow you to see your presentation in different forms. By default, the PowerPoint window opens in **Normal view**, which is the primary view that you use to write, edit, and design your presentation. Normal view is divided into three areas called **panes**: the pane on the left contains the Outline and Slides tabs, the large pane is the Slide pane, and the small pane below the Slide pane is the Notes pane. You move around in each pane using the scroll bars. The PowerPoint window and the specific parts of Normal view are described below.

1. **Click the Start button on the taskbar, point to All Programs, click Microsoft Office, then click Microsoft Office PowerPoint 2007**

   PowerPoint starts and the PowerPoint window opens, as shown in Figure A-4.

Using Figure A-4 as a guide, examine the elements of the PowerPoint window, then find and compare the elements described below:

- The **Ribbon**—a wide (toolbar-like) band that runs across the entire PowerPoint window—is a new feature that organizes all of PowerPoint's primary commands. Each set of primary commands is identified by a **tab**; for example, the Home tab is selected by default as shown in Figure A-4. Commands are further arranged into **groups** on the Ribbon based on their function. So, for example, text formatting commands such as Bold, Underline, and Italic are located on the Home tab, in the Font group.

- The **Outline tab** displays the text of your presentation in the form of an outline, without showing graphics or other visual objects. Using this tab, it is easy to move text on or among slides by dragging text to reorder the information.

- The **Slides tab** displays the slides of your presentation as small images, called **thumbnails**. You can quickly navigate through the slides in your presentation by clicking the thumbnails on this tab. You can also add, delete, or rearrange slides using this tab.

- The **Slide pane** displays the current slide in your presentation.

- The **Notes pane** is used to type text that references a slide's content. You can print these notes and refer to them when you make a presentation or print them as handouts and give them to your audience. The Notes pane is not visible to the audience when you show a slide presentation in Slide Show view.

- The **Quick Access toolbar** provides immediate access to common commands that you use all the time, such as Save, Undo, and Redo. The Quick Access toolbar is always visible no matter which Ribbon tab you select. This toolbar is fully customizable. Click the Customize Quick Access Toolbar button to add or remove commands.

- The **View Shortcuts** on the status bar allow you to switch quickly between PowerPoint views.

- The **status bar**, located at the bottom of the PowerPoint window, shows messages about what you are doing and seeing in PowerPoint, including which slide you are viewing, and the design theme applied to the presentation. In addition, the status bar displays the Zoom slider controls, the **Fit slide to current window button**, and information on other functionality such as signatures and permissions.

- The **Zoom slider**, located in the lower-right corner of the status bar, allows you to zoom the slide in and out quickly.

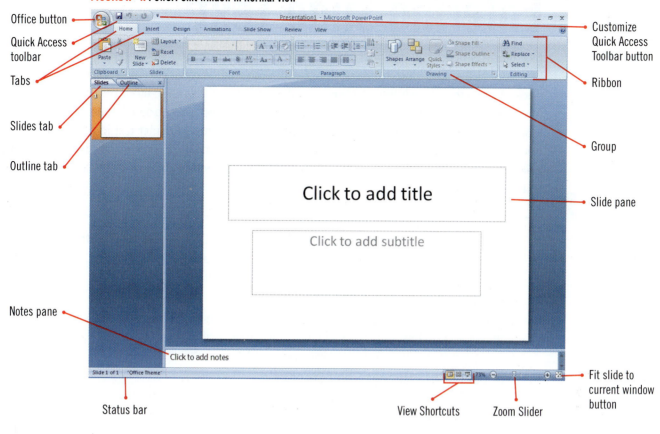

FIGURE A-4: PowerPoint window in Normal view

Office button

Quick Access toolbar

Tabs

Slides tab

Outline tab

Notes pane

Status bar

Customize Quick Access Toolbar button

Ribbon

Group

Slide pane

Fit slide to current window button

View Shortcuts

Zoom Slider

Viewing your presentation in grayscale or black and white

Viewing your presentation in grayscale (using shades of gray) or pure black and white is very useful when you are printing a presentation on a black-and-white printer and you want to make sure your presentation prints correctly. To see how your color presentation looks in grayscale or black and white, click the View tab, then click either the Grayscale or Pure Black and White button. Depending on which button you select, the Grayscale or the Black and White tab

appears and the Ribbon displays different settings that you can customize. If you don't like the way an individual object looks in black and white or grayscale, you can change its color. Right-click the object, point to Black and White Setting or Grayscale Setting (depending on which view you are in), and choose from the options on the submenu.

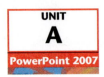

Entering Slide Text

Each time you launch PowerPoint, a new presentation with a blank title slide appears in Normal view. The title slide has two **text placeholders**—boxes with dotted borders—where you enter text. The top text placeholder on the title slide is the **title placeholder**, labeled "Click to add title." The bottom text placeholder on the title slide is the **subtitle text placeholder**, labeled "Click to add subtitle." To enter text in a placeholder, click the placeholder and then type your text. After you enter text in a placeholder, the placeholder becomes a text object. An **object** is any item on a slide that can be modified. Objects are the building blocks that make up a presentation slide. ▨▨ Begin working on your presentation by entering text on the title slide.

STEPS

1. **Move the pointer over the title placeholder labeled "Click to add title" in the Slide pane**
   The pointer changes to I when you move the pointer over the placeholder. In PowerPoint, the pointer often changes shape, depending on the task you are trying to accomplish.

2. **Click the title placeholder in the Slide pane**
   The **insertion point**, a blinking vertical line, indicates where your text appears when you type in the placeholder. A **selection box** with a dashed line border and sizing handles appears around the placeholder, indicating that it is selected and ready to accept text. See Figure A-5.

TROUBLE
If you press a wrong key, press [Backspace] to erase the character.

3. **Type Spring 2011 European Tour Proposal**
   PowerPoint wraps and then center-aligns the title text within the title placeholder, which is now a text object. Notice that the text also appears on the slide thumbnail on the Slides tab.

4. **Click the subtitle text placeholder in the Slide pane**
   The subtitle text placeholder is ready to accept text.

5. **Type Adventure Tour Series, then press [Enter]**
   The insertion point moves to the next line in the text object.

6. **Type Your Name, press [Enter], type Tour Developer-Europe, press [Enter] then type Quest Specialty Travel**
   Notice that the AutoFit Options button ⊞ appears near the text object. The AutoFit Options button on your screen indicates that PowerPoint has automatically decreased the size of all the text in the text object so that it fits inside the text object.

7. **Click the Autofit Options button ⊞, then click Stop Fitting Text to This Placeholder on the shortcut menu**
   The text in the text object changes back to its original size and no longer fits in the text object.

8. **Position I to the right of Series, drag left to select the entire line of text, press [Backspace], then click outside the text object in a blank area of the slide**
   The Adventure Tour Series line of text is deleted and the Autofit Options button closes, as shown in Figure A-6. Clicking a blank area of the slide deselects all selected objects on the slide.

9. **Click the Save button 🖫 on the Quick Access toolbar to open the Save As dialog box, then save the presentation as QuestA in the drive and folder where you store your Data Files**

FIGURE A-5: Title text placeholder ready to accept text

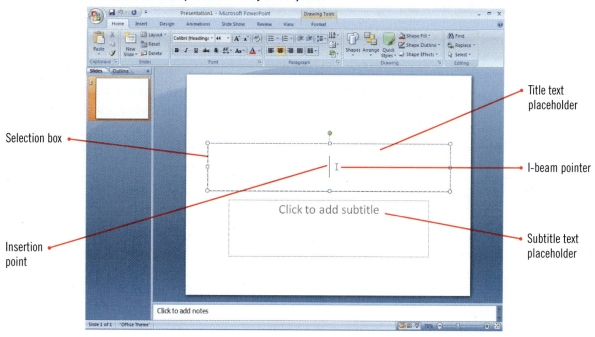

Selection box

Title text placeholder

I-beam pointer

Insertion point

Subtitle text placeholder

FIGURE A-6: Text on title slide

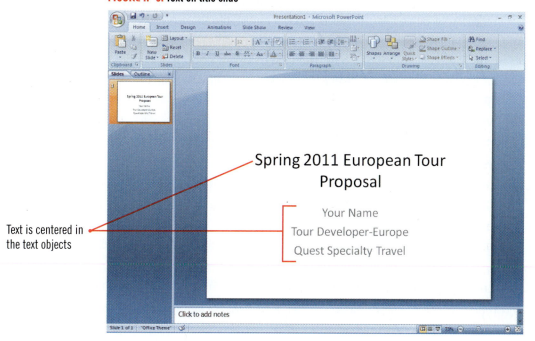

Text is centered in the text objects

Saving fonts with your presentation

When you create a presentation, it uses the fonts that are installed on your computer. If you need to open the presentation on another computer, the fonts might look different if that computer has a different set of fonts. To preserve the look of your presentation on any computer, you can save, or embed, the fonts in your presentation. Click the Office button, then click the PowerPoint Options button. The PowerPoint Options dialog box opens. Click Save in the left pane, then click the Embed fonts in the file check box. Click the Embed all characters option button, then click OK to close the dialog box. Click Save on the Quick Access toolbar. Now the presentation looks the same on any computer that opens it. Using this option, however, significantly increases the size of your presentation, so only use it when necessary. You can freely embed any TrueType font that comes with Windows. You can embed other TrueType fonts only if they have no license restrictions.

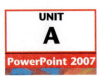

Adding a New Slide

Ordinarily when you add a new slide to a presentation, you have a pretty good idea of what you want the slide to look like. For example, you may want to add a slide that has a title over bulleted text and a picture. To help you add a slide like this quickly and easily, PowerPoint provides nine standard slide layouts. A **slide layout** contains text and object placeholders that are arranged in a specific way on the slide. You have already worked with the Title Slide layout in the previous lesson. In the event that a standard slide layout does not meet your needs, you can modify an existing slide layout or create a brand new, custom slide layout. To continue developing the presentation, you create a slide that defines the QST development goals for the new tour series.

STEPS

1. **Click the New Slide button in the Slides group on the Home tab on the Ribbon**

   A new blank slide (now the current slide) appears as the second slide in your presentation as shown in Figure A-7. The new slide in the Slide pane contains a title placeholder and a content placeholder. A **content placeholder** can be used to insert text or objects such as clip art, tables, or charts. Table A-2 describes the content placeholder icons. Notice that the status bar indicates Slide 2 of 2 and that the Slides tab now contains two slide thumbnails. You can easily change the current slide's layout using the Layout button in the Slides group.

2. **Click the Layout button in the Slides group**

   The Layout gallery opens. Each layout is identified by a descriptive name.

3. **Point to the Two Content slide layout, then click the Two Content slide layout**

   A slide layout with a title placeholder and two content placeholders replaces the Title and Content layout for the current slide.

4. **Type Tour Development Goals, then click the left content placeholder**

   The text you type appears in the title placeholder and the insertion point appears at the top of the left content placeholder.

5. **Type Focus on significant experiences, then press [Enter]**

   A new first-level bullet automatically appears when you press [Enter].

6. **Press [Tab]**

   The new first-level bullet indents and becomes a second-level bullet.

7. **Type Preserve QST values, press [Enter], then click the Decrease List Level button ⊞ in the Paragraph group**

   The Decrease List Level button changes the second-level bullet into a first-level bullet.

8. **Type Price tours reasonably, press [Enter], type Create learning opportunities, press [Enter], then click the Increase List Level button ⊞ in the Paragraph group**

9. **Type Offer local guides, press [Enter], type Provide experts, then click the Save button ⊞ on the Quick Access toolbar**

   The Increase List Level button creates a second-level bullet from a first-level bullet. The Save button saves all of the changes to the file. Compare your screen with Figure A-8.

FIGURE A-7: New blank slide in Normal view

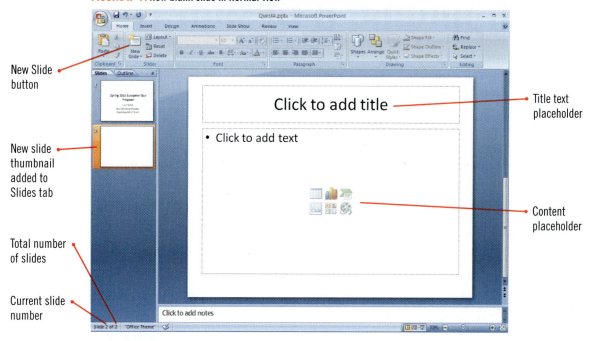

New Slide button

New slide thumbnail added to Slides tab

Total number of slides

Current slide number

Title text placeholder

Content placeholder

FIGURE A-8: New slide with Two Content slide layout

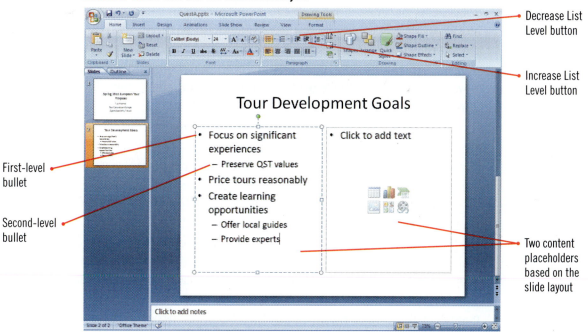

Decrease List Level button

Increase List Level button

First-level bullet

Second-level bullet

Two content placeholders based on the slide layout

TABLE A-2: Content placeholder icons

click this icon	to insert a
	Table
	Graph chart
	Piece of clip art
	Picture from a file
	SmartArt graphic
	Movie or video clip

Applying a Design Theme

PowerPoint provides a number of design themes to help you quickly create a professional and contemporary looking presentation. A design **theme** incorporates sets of colors for fill, line, and shadow, called **theme colors**; fonts for titles and other text, called **theme fonts**; and effects for lines and fills, called **theme effects** to create a cohesive look. In most cases, you would apply one theme to an entire presentation; you can, however, apply multiple themes to the same presentation, or even a different theme on each presentation slide. You can use a design theme as is, or you can alter individual elements of the theme as needed. Unless you need to use a specific design theme, such as a company theme or product design theme, it is faster and easier to use one of the themes supplied with PowerPoint. If you design a custom theme, you can save it to use in the future. 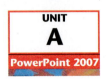 You decide to change the default design theme in the presentation to a new one.

STEPS

1. **Click the Slide 1 thumbnail on the Slides tab**

   Slide 1, the title slide, appears in the Slide pane.

2. **Click the Design tab on the Ribbon, then point to the Civic theme in the Themes group as shown in Figure A-9**

   The Design tab appears and a live preview of the Civic theme is displayed on the slide. A **live preview** allows you to see how your changes affect the slides before actually making the change. The live preview lasts about one minute and then your slide reverts back to its original state. The first (far left) theme thumbnail identifies the current theme applied to the presentation, in this case, the default design theme called the Office Theme. Depending on your monitor resolution and screen size, you can see between five and seven design themes visible in the Themes group. However, there are a total of 20 standard built-in themes available to use.

3. **Slowly move your pointer ⌖ over the other design themes, then click the Themes group down scroll arrow once**

   A live preview of the theme appears on the slide each time you pass your pointer over the theme thumbnails, and a ScreenTip identifies the theme names.

4. **Move ⌖ over the design themes, then click the Metro theme**

   The Metro design theme is applied to all the slides in the presentation. Notice the new slide background color, graphic elements, fonts, and text color. You decide that this theme isn't right for this presentation.

QUICK TIP

One way to apply multiple themes to the same presentation is to click the Slide Sorter button in the status bar, select a slide or a group of slides, then click the theme.

5. **Click the More button ⤓ in the Themes group**

   The Themes gallery window opens. At the top of the gallery window in the This Presentation section are the current theme(s) applied to the presentation. Notice that just the Metro theme is listed here because when you changed the theme in the last step, you replaced the default theme with the Metro theme. The Built-In section identifies all of the standard themes that come with PowerPoint.

6. **Right-click the Solstice theme in the Themes group, then click Apply to Selected Slides**

   The Solstice theme is applied only to Slide 1. You like the Solstice theme better and decide to apply it to both slides.

7. **Right-click the Solstice theme in the Themes group, then click Apply to All Slides**

   The Solstice theme is applied to both slides. Preview the other slide in the presentation to see how it looks.

8. **Click the Next Slide button ⤓ at the bottom of the vertical scroll bar**

   Compare your screen to Figure A-10.

9. **Click the Previous Slide button ⤒ at the bottom of the vertical scroll bar, then save your changes**

FIGURE A-9: Slide showing a different design theme

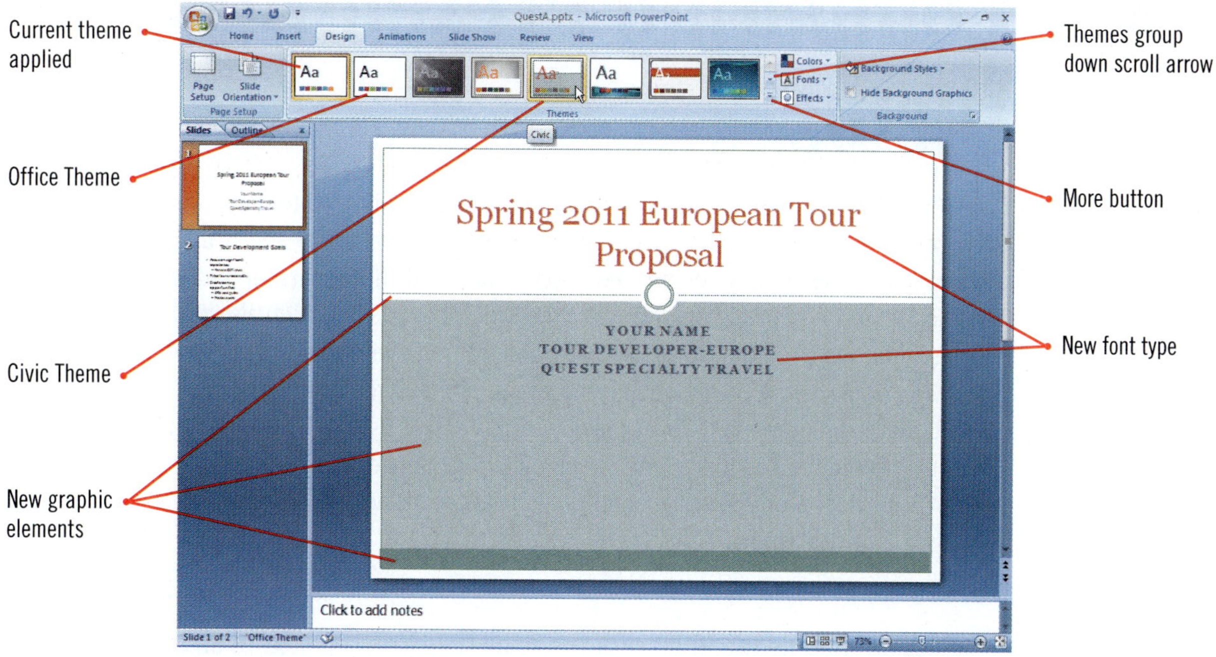

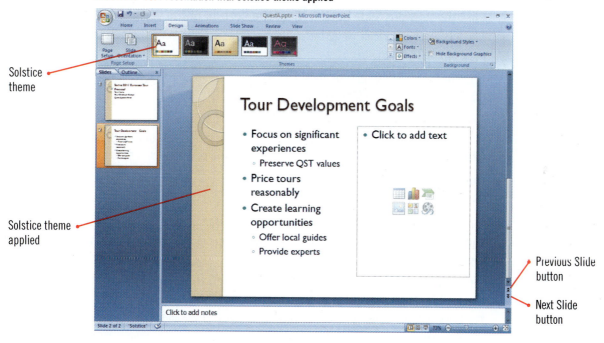

Current theme applied

Office Theme

Civic Theme

New graphic elements

Themes group down scroll arrow

More button

New font type

FIGURE A-10: Presentation with Solstice theme applied

Solstice theme

Solstice theme applied

Previous Slide button

Next Slide button

Customizing themes

You are not limited to using the standard themes PowerPoint provides; you can also modify a theme to create your own custom theme. For example, you might want to incorporate your company's colors on the slide background of the presentation or be able to type using fonts your company uses for brand recognition. To modify an existing theme, you can change the color theme, font theme, or the effects theme and then save it for future use by clicking the Themes group More button, then clicking Save Current Theme. You also have the ability to create a new font theme or a new color theme from scratch by clicking the Theme Fonts button or the Theme Colors button and then clicking Create New Theme Fonts or Create New Theme Colors. You work in the Create New Theme Fonts or Create New Theme Colors dialog box to define the custom theme fonts or colors.

Comparing Presentation Views

PowerPoint has four basic views: Normal view, Slide Sorter view, Notes Page view, and Slide Show view. Each PowerPoint view displays your presentation in a different way and is used for different purposes. Normal view is the primary editing view where you add text, graphics, and other elements to the slides. Slide Sorter view is primarily used to rearrange slides, however, you can also add slide effects and design themes in this view. You use Notes Page view to type notes you want to remember about each slide. Slide Show view displays your presentation filling the computer screen and is the view used to give a presentation. To move easily among three of the PowerPoint views, use the View Shortcuts buttons located in the Status bar next to the Zoom slider. All PowerPoint views can be accessed using the View tab on the Ribbon. Table A-3 provides a brief description of the PowerPoint views. Examine each of the PowerPoint views, starting with Normal view.

STEPS

1. Click the Outline tab, then click the small slide icon next to Slide 2 in the Outline tab
   The text for Slide 2 is selected in the Outline tab and Slide 2 appears in the Slide pane as shown in Figure A-11. Notice that the status bar identifies the number of the slide you are viewing, the total number of slides in the presentation, and the name of the applied design theme.

2. Click the Previous Slide button at the bottom of the vertical scroll bar
   Slide 1 appears in the Slide pane. The scroll box in the vertical scroll bar moves back up the scroll bar.

3. Click the Slides tab
   Thumbnails of the slides in your presentation appear again on the Slides tab. Since the Slides tab is narrower than the Outline tab, the Slide pane enlarges.

   > **QUICK TIP**
   > You can also switch between views using the commands in the Presentation Views group on the View tab.

4. Click the Slide Sorter button on the status bar
   A thumbnail of each slide in the presentation appears as shown in Figure A-12. You can examine the flow of your slides and drag any slide or group of slides to rearrange the order of the slides in the presentation.

5. Double-click Slide 1 in Slide Sorter view
   Slide 1 appears in Normal view.

6. Click the Slide Show button on the status bar
   The first slide fills the entire screen. In this view, you can practice running through your slides as they would appear in the slide show.

   > **QUICK TIP**
   > You can also press [Enter] or [Spacebar] to advance the slide show.

7. Click the left mouse button to advance through the slides one at a time until you see a black slide, then click once more to return to Normal view
   The black slide at the end of the slide show indicates that the slide show is finished. At the end of a slide show you automatically return to the slide and PowerPoint view you were in before you ran the slide show, in this case Slide 1 in Normal view.

8. Click the View tab on the Ribbon, then click the Notes Page button in the Presentation Views group
   Notes Page view appears, showing a reduced image of the current slide above a large text placeholder. You can enter text in this placeholder and then print the notes page for your own use.

9. Click the Normal button in the Presentation Views group

FIGURE A-11: Normal view with the outline tab displayed

Outline tab

Slides tab

Slide icon

Design theme name

Normal button

Slide Sorter button

Slide Show button

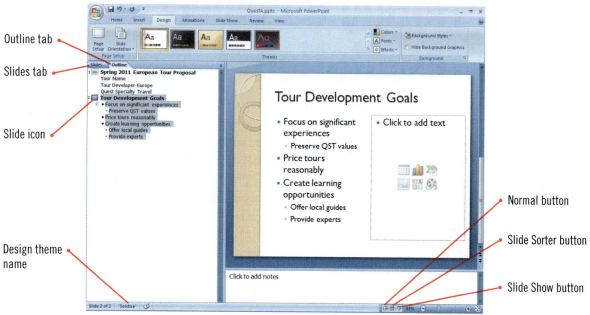

FIGURE A-12: Slide Sorter view

Slide 1

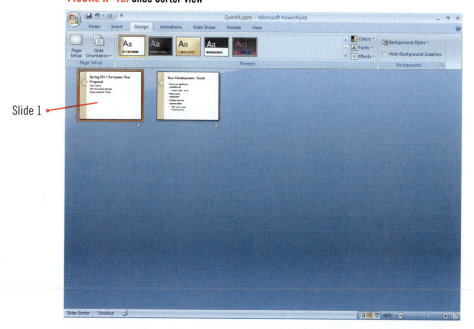

TABLE A-3: PowerPoint views

view name	button	button name	description
Normal		Normal	Displays the Outline and Slides tabs, the Slide pane, and the Notes pane at the same time; use this view to work on your presentation's content, layout, and notes concurrently
Slide Sorter		Slide Sorter	Displays thumbnails of all slides in the order in which they appear in your presentation; use this view to rearrange and add special effects to your slides
Slide Show		Slide Show	Displays your presentation as an electronic slide show
Notes Page	(no View Shortcut button)		Displays a reduced image of the current slide above a large text box where you can enter or view notes

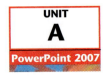
Printing a PowerPoint Presentation

You print your presentation when you want to review your work or when you have completed it and want a hard copy. Reviewing your presentation at different stages of development gives you a better perspective of the overall flow and feel of the presentation. You can also preview your presentation to see exactly how each slide looks before you print the presentation. When you are finished working on your presentation, even if it is not yet complete, you can close the presentation file and exit PowerPoint. You are done working on the tour presentation for now. You save and preview the presentation, then you print the slides and notes pages of the presentation so you can review them later. Before leaving for the day, you close the file and exit PowerPoint.

STEPS

1. **Click the Office button 📎, point to Print, then click Print Preview**

   The Print Preview window opens as shown in Figure A-13. Notice the Print Preview tab appears on the Ribbon, which now displays associated commands for the Print Preview window.

> **QUICK TIP**
>
> To quickly print the presentation with the current Print options, add the Quick Print button to the Quick Access toolbar.

2. **Click the Next Page button in the Preview group, then click the Print button in the Print group**

   You view Slide 2 before opening the Print dialog box. In the Print dialog box, you can specify what you want to print (slides, handouts, notes pages, or outline), the slide range, the number of copies to print, as well as other print options. The default options for the available printer are selected in the dialog box.

3. **Click the Slides option button in the Print range section of the dialog box to select it, type 2 to print only the second slide, then click OK**

   The second slide prints. To save paper when you are reviewing your slides, you can print in handout format, which lets you print up to nine slides per page.

4. **Click the Close Print Preview button in the Preview group, click the Office button 📎, then click Print**

   The Print dialog box opens again. The options you choose in the Print dialog box remain there until you close the presentation.

> **QUICK TIP**
>
> To print slides appropriate in size for overhead transparencies, click the Design tab, click the Page Setup button in the Page Setup group, click the Slides sized for list arrow, then click Overhead.

5. **Click the All option button in the Print range section, click the Print what list arrow, click Handouts, click the Slides per page list arrow in the Handouts section, then click 3**

6. **Click the Color/grayscale list arrow, click Pure Black and White as shown in Figure A-14, then click OK**

   The presentation prints as handouts showing slide thumbnails next to blank lines. Using the Handouts with three slides per page printing option is a great way to print your presentation when you want to provide a way for audience members to take notes. Printing in pure black and white prints without any gray tones and can save printer toner.

7. **Click the Office button 📎, then click Close**

   If you have made changes to your presentation, a Microsoft PowerPoint alert box opens asking you if you want to save changes you have made to your presentation file.

8. **Click Yes, if necessary, to close the alert box**

   Your presentation closes.

9. **Click the Office button 📎, then click the Exit PowerPoint button**

   The PowerPoint program closes, and you return to the Windows desktop.

FIGURE A-13: Print Preview window

Print Preview tab

Print button

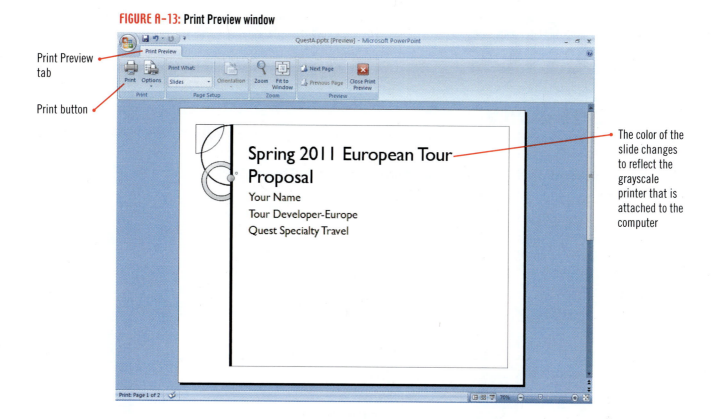

The color of the slide changes to reflect the grayscale printer that is attached to the computer

FIGURE A-14: Print dialog box with Handouts selected

Your printer name may be different

Slides option button

Click to select an item to print

Color/grayscale list arrow

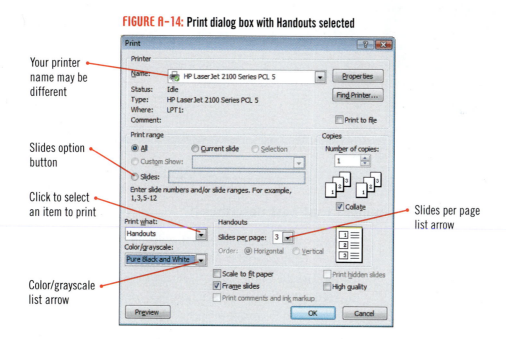

Slides per page list arrow

Animating in PowerPoint

Providing emphasis to the information in your presentation can help your audience retain that information. Animating text and other objects is one dramatic way to provide emphasis. Animations make a presentation engaging and enjoyable to watch. You can animate text, shapes, diagrams, charts, and other objects, which provides you a wide variety of options to create a dynamic presentation. You can also add interesting effects to the way slides are presented or transition on the screen. Types of animation effects include flying in or out, fading, and changing color.

Practice

If you have a SAM user profile, you may have access to hands-on instruction, practice, and assessment of the skills covered in this unit. Log in to your SAM account (http://sam2007.course.com/) to launch any assigned training activities or exams that relate to the skills covered in this unit.

▼ CONCEPTS REVIEW

Label each element of the PowerPoint window shown in Figure A-15.

FIGURE A-15

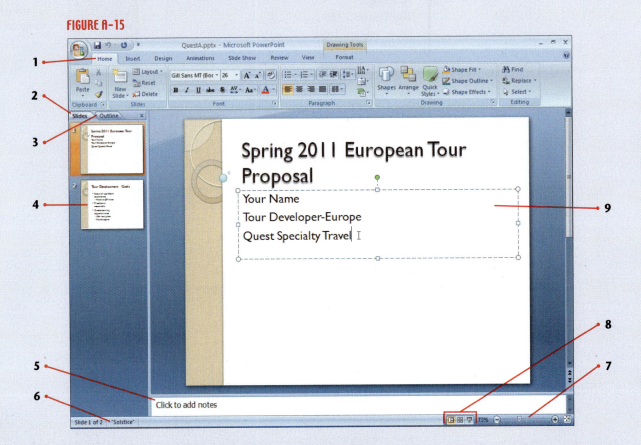

Match each term with the statement that best describes it.

10. Ribbon
11. Normal view
12. Slide Sorter view
13. Zoom slider
14. Notes pane

a. A view that displays slides as thumbnails
b. Used to organize all of PowerPoint's commands
c. Displays the Outline and Slides tabs, as well as the Slide and Notes panes
d. Used to type text that references slide content
e. Allows you to change the size of the slide in the window

Select the best answer from the list of choices.

15. When you type text in a placeholder, it becomes:

a. A label

b. A text object

c. A text processing object

d. A selection box

16. The buttons you use to switch between the PowerPoint views in the status bar are called:

a. Toolbar buttons

b. View buttons

c. PowerPoint buttons

d. View Shortcuts

17. All of the following are PowerPoint views, except:

a. Notes Page view

b. Outline Page view

c. Normal view

d. Slide Sorter view

18. What does the slide layout do in a presentation?

a. A slide layout defines how all the elements on a slide are arranged.

b. A slide layout automatically applies all the objects you can use on a slide.

c. The slide layout puts all your slides in order.

d. The slide layout enables you to apply a template to the presentation.

19. The view that fills the entire screen with each slide in the presentation is called:

a. Presentation view

b. Slide Sorter view

c. Slide Show view

d. Slide view

20. According to the unit, which of the following is not a guideline for planning a presentation?

a. Determine how much time you need to give the presentation.

b. Determine the purpose of the presentation.

c. Determine what you want to produce when the presentation is finished.

d. Determine which type of output you need to best convey your message.

21. Other than the Slide pane, where else can you enter slide text?

a. Slides tab

b. Outline tab

c. Tab Preview

d. Notes Page view

▼ SKILLS REVIEW

1. Start PowerPoint and examine the PowerPoint window.

a. Start PowerPoint, if necessary.

b. Identify as many elements of the PowerPoint window as you can without referring to the unit material.

c. Be able to describe the purpose or function of each element.

d. For any elements you cannot identify, refer to the unit.

2. Enter slide text.

a. In the Slide pane in Normal view, enter the text **Historic Middle Fork Land & Camps Protection Proposal** in the title placeholder. Refer to Figure A-16 as you complete the slide.

b. In the subtitle text placeholder, enter **Historic Lands Preservation Society**

FIGURE A-16: Slide 1 of the completed presentation

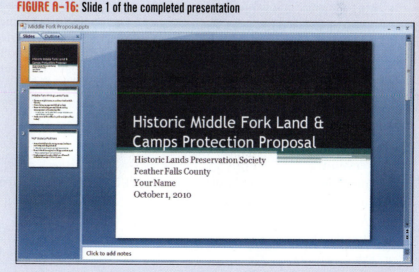

    c. On the next line of the placeholder, enter **Feather Falls County**.

    d. On the next line of the placeholder, enter **Your Name**.

    e. On the next line of the placeholder, enter **October 1, 2010**. Let PowerPoint AutoFit the text in the text object.

    f. Deselect the text object.

    g. Save the presentation using the filename **Middle Fork Proposal** to the drive and folder where you store your Data Files.

3. Add new slides.

    a. Create a new slide.

    b. Using Figure A-17, enter text on the slide.

    c. Create another new slide.

    d. Using Figure A-18, enter text on the slide.

    e. Save your changes.

4. Apply a design theme.

    a. Click the Design tab.

    b. Click the Themes group More button, then point to all of the themes.

    c. Locate the Verve theme, then apply it to all the slides.

    d. Move to Slide 1.

    e. Locate the Urban theme, then apply it to Slide 1.

    f. Apply the Urban theme to all of the slides in the presentation.

    g. Use the Next Slide button to move to Slide 3, then save your changes.

5. Compare presentation views.

    a. Click the View tab.

    b. Click the Slide Sorter button in the Presentation Views group.

    c. Click the Notes Page button in the Presentation Views group, then click the Previous Slide button twice.

    d. Click the Normal button in the Presentation Views group, then click the Slide Show button.

    e. Click until a black screen appears, then click to end the presentation.

    f. Save your changes.

6. Print and close a presentation, and exit PowerPoint.

    a. Print Slide 1 as slides in grayscale. (*Hint*: Click the Current slide option button in the Print dialog box.)

    b. Print all the slides as handouts, 3 slides per page, in pure black and white.

    c. Print the presentation outline.

    d. Close the file, saving your changes.

    e. Exit PowerPoint.

FIGURE A-17

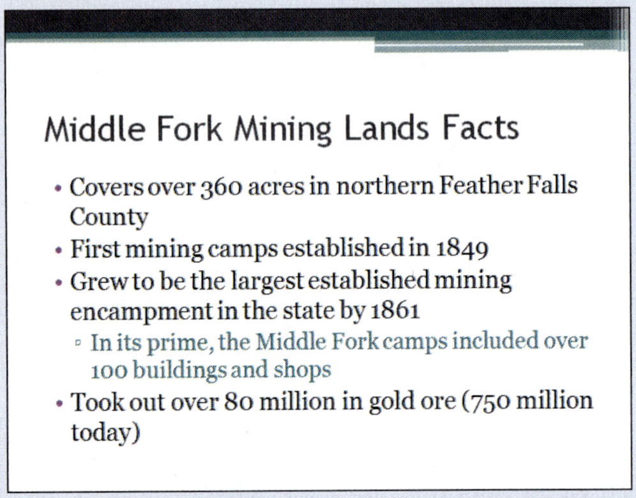

Middle Fork Mining Lands Facts

- Covers over 360 acres in northern Feather Falls County
- First mining camps established in 1849
- Grew to be the largest established mining encampment in the state by 1861
  - In its prime, the Middle Fork camps included over 100 buildings and shops
- Took out over 80 million in gold ore (750 million today)

FIGURE A-18

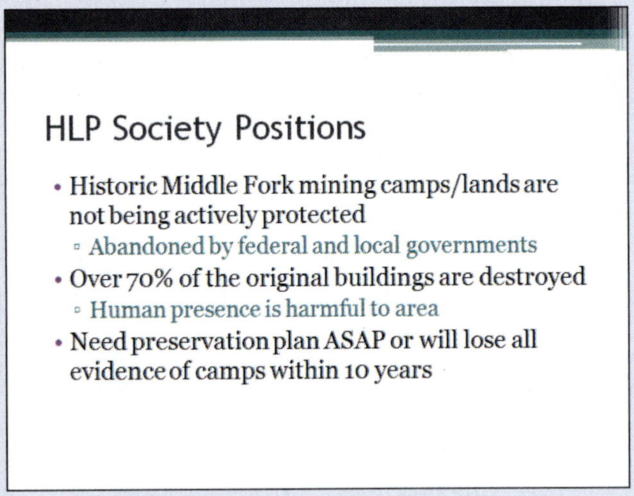

HLP Society Positions

- Historic Middle Fork mining camps/lands are not being actively protected
  - Abandoned by federal and local governments
- Over 70% of the original buildings are destroyed
  - Human presence is harmful to area
- Need preservation plan ASAP or will lose all evidence of camps within 10 years

▼ INDEPENDENT CHALLENGE 1

You work for Resource Industries, a business that that offers environmental hazard clean up and project management. In an effort to expand the business, your boss has asked you to create a sales presentation that describes the services Resource Industries offers.

a. Start PowerPoint.

b. In the title placeholder on Slide 1, type **Resource Industries**

c. In the sub-title placeholder, type **Professional & Client Services**, press **[Enter]**, type **Your Name**, press **[Enter]**, then type **Today's Date**

d. Apply the Equity design theme to the slide.

e. Save your presentation with the filename **Resource Industries** to the drive and folder where you store your Data Files.

f. Use Figures A-19 and A-20 to add two more slides to your presentation. (*Hint*: Slide 2 uses the Comparison layout.)

g. Use the commands on the View tab to switch between all of PowerPoint's views.

h. Preview the presentation using the Print Preview command, print the presentation using the Slides option, save and close the file, then exit PowerPoint.

FIGURE A-19

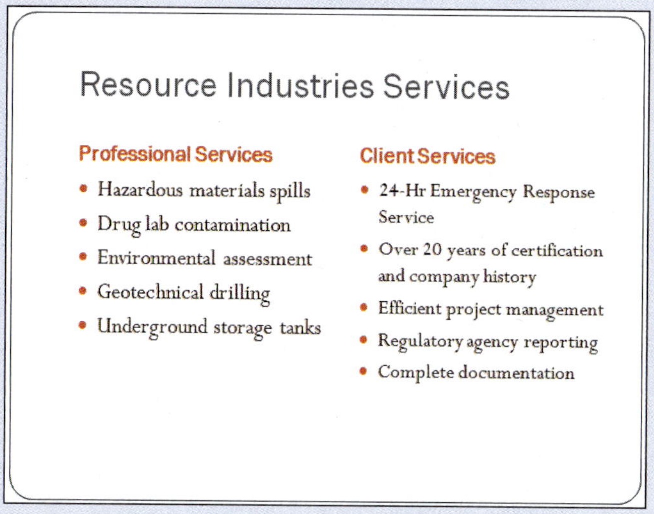

Resource Industries Services

Professional Services
- Hazardous materials spills
- Drug lab contamination
- Environmental assessment
- Geotechnical drilling
- Underground storage tanks

Client Services
- 24-Hr Emergency Response Service
- Over 20 years of certification and company history
- Efficient project management
- Regulatory agency reporting
- Complete documentation

FIGURE A-20

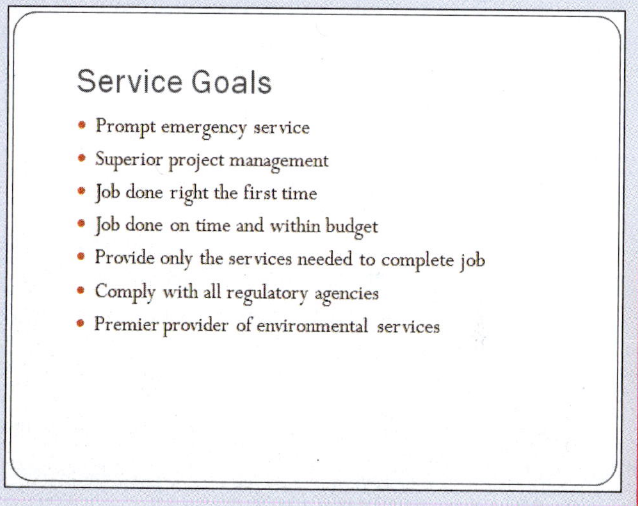

Service Goals
- Prompt emergency service
- Superior project management
- Job done right the first time
- Job done on time and within budget
- Provide only the services needed to complete job
- Comply with all regulatory agencies
- Premier provider of environmental services

▼ INDEPENDENT CHALLENGE 2

You have recently been promoted to national sales manager at Windman Power Industries, which manufactures personal watercraft, including items such as paddle boats, canoes, kayaks, sail boats, and rafts. Part of your job is to present company sales figures at a yearly sales meeting. Use the following information as the basis for units sold nationally in your presentation: 797 canoes, 1302 kayaks, 421 paddle boats, 4219 sail boats, 230 rafts. Assume that Windman Power has five sales regions throughout the country: West, East, South, Midwest, and Northeast. Also, assume overall sales rose 22% during the last year and gross sales reached $230 million. The presentation should have at least five slides.

a. Spend some time planning the slides of your presentation. What is the best way to show the information provided? What other information could you add that might be useful for this presentation?

b. Start PowerPoint.

c. Give the presentation an appropriate title on the title slide and enter today's date and your name in the subtitle placeholder.

d. Add slides and enter appropriate slide text.

▼ INDEPENDENT CHALLENGE 2 (CONTINUED)

e. On the last slide of the presentation, include the following information:

Windman Power Industries

PO Box 777

West Chester, IN 39022

f. Apply a design theme. A typical slide might look like the one shown in Figure A-21.

Advanced Challenge Exercise

- Open the Notes Page view.
- Add notes to three slides.
- Print the Notes Page view for the presentation.

g. Switch views. Run through the slide show at least once.

h. Save your presentation with the filename **Windman** where you store your Data Files.

i. Close the presentation and exit PowerPoint.

FIGURE A-21

An Overall View

Sales Figures
- This year's results!
  - $230 million gross sales
- Comparison to last year
  - $65 million increase in overall sales
- Region by region
  - West-up by 12%
  - East-down by 5%
  - Northeast-up by 6%
  - South-up by 11%
  - Midwest-up by 7%

National Sales
- Product Sales
  - Canoes- 797 units
  - Kayaks- 1302 units
  - Paddle boats- 421 units
  - Sail boats- 4219 units
  - Rafts- 230 units

▼ INDEPENDENT CHALLENGE 3

You work for ThaiMade Trade Co., an emerging company that exports goods from Thailand. The company wants to expand its business globally. The Internet marketing director has asked you to plan and create a PowerPoint presentation that he will use to convey an expanded Internet service that will target Western countries. This new Internet service will allow customers to purchase all kinds of Thai made goods. Sample items for sale include silver and turquoise jewelry, hand crafts, folk art, terra cotta kitchenware, wooden decorative items, and bamboo furniture. Your presentation should contain product information and pricing. Use the Internet, if possible, to research information that will help you formulate your ideas. The presentation should have at least five slides.

a. Spend some time planning the slides of your presentation. What information would a consumer need to have to purchase items on this Web site?

b. Start PowerPoint.

c. Give the presentation an appropriate title on the title slide and enter today's date and your name in the subtitle placeholder.

d. Add slides and enter appropriate slide text.

e. On the last slide of the presentation, type the following information:

ThaiMade Trade Co.

Satrani Condominium Room 214

36/980 Moo 5 Sethup Sub District, Muang district,

Chiangmai 50208 Thailand

Tel/Fax: +90-49-39850 Hotline: (03)249347

FIGURE A-22

Fine Jewelry Product List

Silver Jewelry	Turquoise Jewelry
☐ Bracelets	☐ Bracelets
☐ Necklaces	☐ Necklaces
☐ Rings	☐ Rings
☐ Earrings	☐ Earrings
☐ Watches	
☐ Pendants	

f. Apply a design theme. A typical slide might look like the one shown in Figure A-22.

g. Switch views. Run through the slide show at least once.

h. Save your presentation with the filename **ThaiMade** where you store your Data Files.

i. Close the presentation and exit PowerPoint.

▼ REAL LIFE INDEPENDENT CHALLENGE

Every year your college holds a large fund raising event to support a local charity. This year the Student Advisory Committee has chosen to help the East Hills Cerebral Palsy Center. To help them decide what kind of an event to hold this year, the Advisory Committee has appealed to the student body for fund raising ideas. Your idea is to host a regional Bar-B-Q cook off competition that includes local and professional cooking teams. Your idea was chosen as one of the finalist ideas and you need to present your proposal in a meeting of the Advisory Committee.

a. Spend some time planning the slides of your presentation. Assume the following: there are four competition categories (beef brisket, pork shoulder, pork ribs, and chicken); the competition is a two day event; event advertising will be city- and region-wide; local music groups will also be invited; there will be a kids section with games; the event will be held on the college football field. Use the Internet, if possible, to research information that will help you formulate your ideas.

b. Start PowerPoint.

c. Give the presentation an appropriate title on the title slide and enter your name and today's date in the subtitle placeholder.

d. Add slides and enter appropriate slide text. A typical slide might look like the one shown in Figure A-23.

e. View the presentation.

f. Save your presentation with the filename **Bar-B-Q Cookoff** where you store your Data Files.

g. Close the presentation and exit PowerPoint.

FIGURE A-23

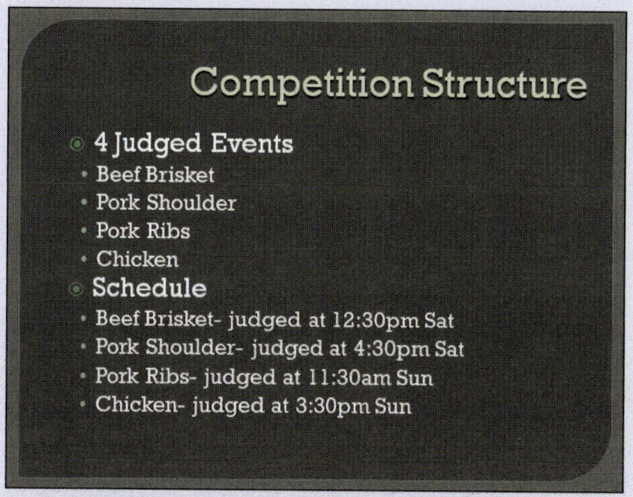

Competition Structure

- 4 Judged Events
  - Beef Brisket
  - Pork Shoulder
  - Pork Ribs
  - Chicken
- Schedule
  - Beef Brisket- judged at 12:30pm Sat
  - Pork Shoulder- judged at 4:30pm Sat
  - Pork Ribs- judged at 11:30am Sun
  - Chicken- judged at 3:30pm Sun

▼ VISUAL WORKSHOP

Create the presentation shown in Figures A-24 and A-25. Make sure you include your name on the title slide. Save the presentation as **PackJet Project Tests** where you store your Data Files. Print the slides.

FIGURE A-24

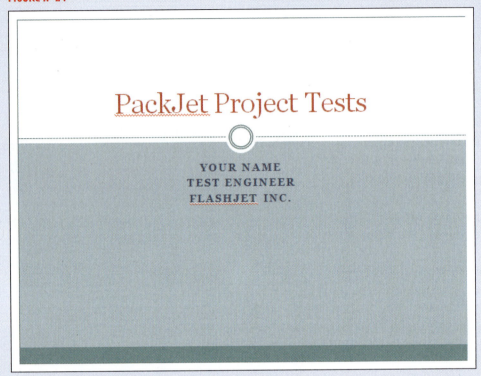

FIGURE A-25

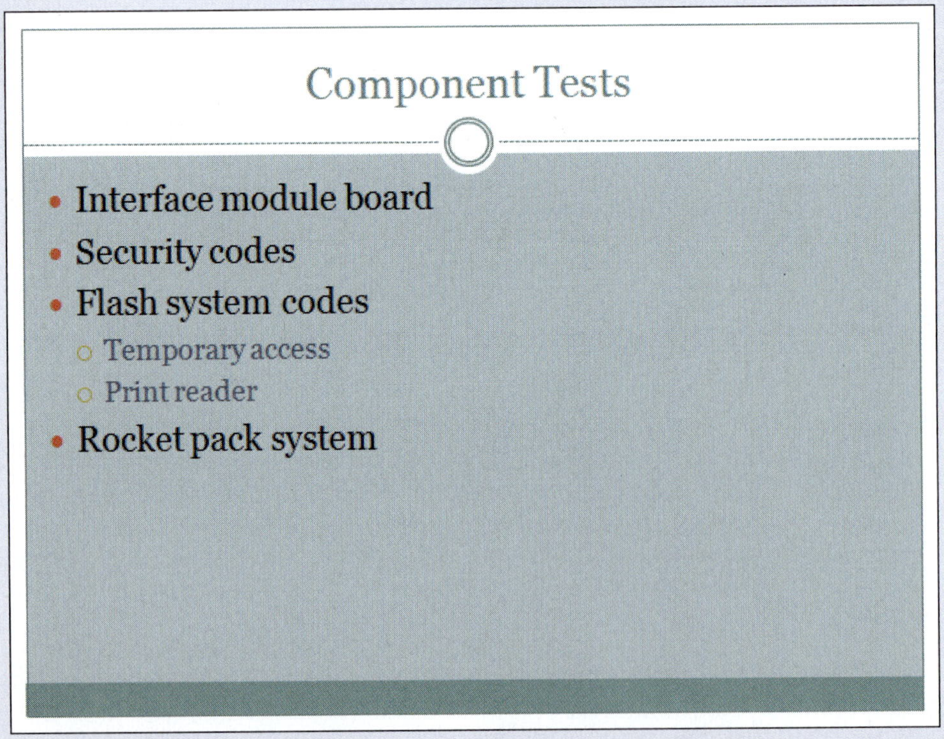

Modifying a Presentation

Files You Will Need:

PPT B-1.pptx
PPT B-2.pptx
PPT B-3.pptx
PPT B-4.pptx
PPT B-5.pptx

In the previous unit you learned how to enter slide text, add a new slide, and apply a design theme. Now, you are ready to take the next step in creating professional-looking presentations by learning to format text and work with drawn objects. In this unit, you'll enter text in the Outline tab, format text, draw and modify objects, add slide footer information, and check the spelling in the presentation. You continue working on the European tour proposal presentation for Ellen Latsky.

OBJECTIVES

Enter text in the Outline tab

Format text

Convert text to SmartArt

Insert and modify shapes

Edit and duplicate shapes

Align and group objects

Add slide headers and footers

Check spelling in a presentation

Entering Text in the Outline Tab

You can enter presentation text by typing directly on the slide in the Slide pane, or, if you'd rather focus on the presentation text without worrying about the layout, you can enter text in the Outline tab. The outline is organized so that the headings, or slide titles, appear at the top of the outline. Beneath the title, each subpoint, or each line of bulleted text, appears as one or more indented lines under the title. Each indent in the outline creates another level of bulleted text on the slide. You switch to the Outline tab to enter text for two more slides in the European tour proposal presentation. Begin by entering more text using the Outline tab.

STEPS

QUICK TIP

To convert an older presentation to PowerPoint 2007 format, open the presentation in PowerPoint 2007, click the Office button, click Convert, then click OK in the dialog box.

1. **Start PowerPoint, open the presentation PPT B-1.pptx from the drive and folder where you store your Data Files, save it as QuestB, click the View tab on the Ribbon, then click the Arrange All button in the Window group**

   The Slide pane, Notes pane, and Slide and Outline tabs are now in their own window with the presentation title at the top.

2. **Click the Slide 2 thumbnail in the Slides tab, then click the Outline tab**

   The Outline tab enlarges to display the text that is on the slides. The slide icon and the text for Slide 2 are highlighted, indicating that it's selected. Notice the number 1 that appears to the left of the first-level bullet for Slide 2, indicating that there are multiple content placeholders on the slide.

3. **Click the Home tab on the Ribbon, click the New Slide button list arrow in the Slides group, then click Title and Content**

   A new slide, Slide 3, with the Title and Content layout appears as the current slide below Slide 2. A blinking insertion point appears next to the new slide in the Outline tab. See Figure B-1. Text that you enter next to a slide icon becomes the title for that slide.

4. **Type Focus Group Data Analyzed, press [Enter], then press [Tab]**

   When you first press [Enter] you create a new slide, but because you want to enter bulleted text on Slide 3 you press [Tab] so that the text you type is entered as bullet text on Slide 3.

5. **Type Trends, press [Enter], type Major Findings, press [Enter], type Conclusions, then press [Enter]**

   The last time you press [Enter], you create a bullet that has no text at the end of this slide.

6. **Press [Shift][Tab]**

   The last bullet that was created on Slide 3 becomes a new slide.

QUICK TIP

Pressing [Ctrl][Enter] while the cursor is in the text object creates a new slide with the same layout as the previous slide.

7. **Type Tour Strategy Objectives, press [Ctrl][Enter], then type the rest of the information on Slide 4 as shown in Figure B-2**

   Pressing [Ctrl][Enter] while the cursor is in the title text object moves the cursor into the content placeholder. Make sure you misspell the word "Utilze" as shown on the slide.

8. **Position the pointer on the Slide 4 icon in the Outline tab**

   The pointer changes to ✥. Slide 4 is out of order.

9. **Drag the Slide 4 icon up until a horizontal indicator line appears above the Slide 3 icon, then release the mouse button**

   The fourth slide moves up and switches places with the third slide.

10. **Click the Slides tab, then save your work**

    The Outline tab closes and the Slides tab is now visible in the window.

FIGURE B-1: Outline tab open showing new slide

Outline tab

New slide

Text you type here becomes the slide title

Drag the pane divider line to change the width of the Outline tab

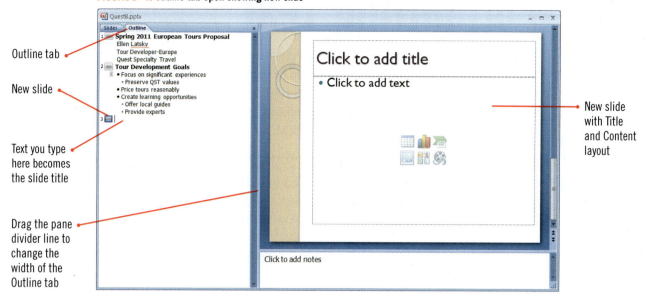

New slide with Title and Content layout

FIGURE B-2: Slide 4 with new information

Make sure you misspell this word

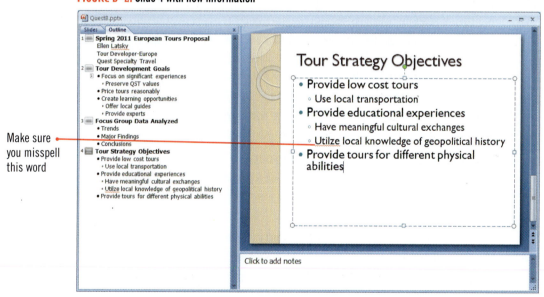

Setting permissions

In PowerPoint, you can set specific access permissions for people who review or edit your work, so you have better control over your content. For example, you may want to give a user permission to edit or change your presentation but not allow them to print it. You can also restrict a user by permitting them to view the presentation, without the ability to edit or print the presentation, or you can give the user full access or control of the presentation. To use this feature, you first have to install the Windows Rights Management Services software using the Add or Remove Programs feature in the Control Panel, which installs the Restrict Permissions feature on the Office button. Then, to set user access permissions, click the Office button, point to Prepare, point to Restrict Permission, then click the appropriate option.

Formatting Text

Once you have entered and edited the text in your presentation, you can modify the way the text looks to emphasize your message. Important text should be highlighted in some way to distinguish it from other text or objects on the slide. For example, if you have two text objects on the same slide, you could draw attention to one text object by changing its color, font, or size. In order to enhance the European tour proposal presentation, you format text on Slide 4.

STEPS

QUICK TIP
Open the PowerPoint Options dialog box to set the option to show or hide the Mini toolbar.

1. **Click the Slide 4 thumbnail in the Slides tab, then double-click Trends in the text object**

   The word Trends is selected and a small semitransparent Mini toolbar appears above the text. The **Mini toolbar** contains basic text formatting commands, such as bold and italic, and appears when you select text using the mouse. This toolbar makes it quick and easy to format text, especially when the Home tab is not open.

2. **Move the pointer over the Mini toolbar, click the Font Color button list arrow $\underline{A}$, then click the Dark Red color box under Standard Colors**

   The text changes color to dark red as shown in Figure B-3. As soon as you move the pointer over the Mini toolbar, the toolbar becomes clearly visible. When you click the Font Color button list arrow, the Font Color gallery appears showing the Theme Colors and Standard Colors. Notice that the Font Color button on the Mini toolbar and the Font Color button on the Home tab change color to reflect the new color choice.

QUICK TIP
You can also select the entire text object by clicking its border when the text object is already selected.

3. **Click outside the text object in a blank area of the slide, press and hold [Shift], click the text object, then release [Shift]**

   A selection box with small circles and squares called **sizing handles** appears around the text object. The entire text object is selected, and changes you make now affect all of the text in the text object. If you click a text object without pressing [Shift], a dotted selection box appears, indicating that the object is active and ready to accept text, but the text object itself is not selected. When the whole text object is selected, you can change its size, shape, or other attributes. Changing the color of the text helps emphasize it.

4. **Click the Font Color button $\underline{A}$ in the Font group**

   All of the text in the text object changes to the dark red color.

5. **Click the Font list arrow in the Font group**

   A list of available fonts opens with Gill Sans MT, the current font used in the text object, selected at the top of the list with the Theme Fonts.

6. **Click Arial Narrow**

   The Arial Narrow font replaces the original font in the text object. Notice that as you move the pointer over the font names in the font list the text on the slide displays a live preview of the different font choices.

7. **Click the Text Shadow button $\boxed{S}$ in the Font group, click the Change Case button $\boxed{Aa}$ in the Font group, then click UPPERCASE**

   All of the text now displays a gray shadow and is uppercase.

8. **Click the Bullets button list arrow $\boxed{\equiv}$ in the Paragraph group, click None, then click the Center button $\boxed{\equiv}$ in the Paragraph group**

   The bullets no longer appear next to the text and the text moves to the center of the text box. Compare your screen to Figure B-4.

9. **Click a blank area of the slide outside the text object to deselect it, then save your work**

FIGURE B-3: Selected word with Mini toolbar open

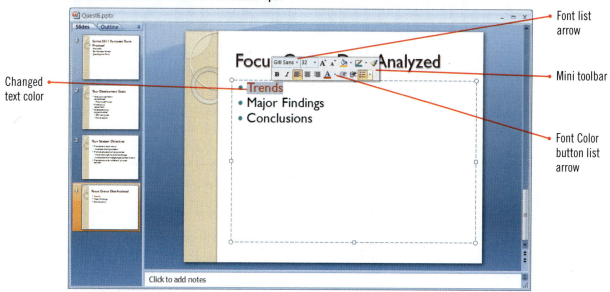

Changed text color

Font list arrow

Mini toolbar

Font Color button list arrow

FIGURE B-4: Formatted text

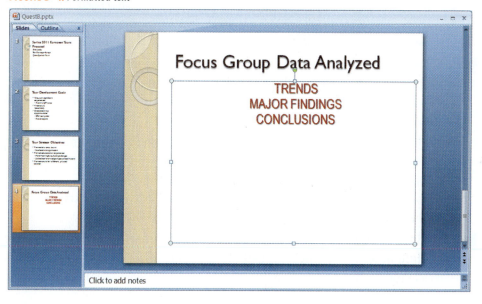

Replacing text and fonts

As you review your presentation, you may decide to replace certain text or fonts throughout the entire presentation using the Replace command. Text can be a word, phrase, or sentence. To replace specific text, click the Home tab on the Ribbon, then click the Replace button in the Editing group. In the Replace dialog box, enter the text you want to replace then enter the text you want to use as its replacement. You can also use the Replace command to replace one font for another. Simply click the Replace button list arrow in the Editing group, then click Replace Fonts to open the Replace Font dialog box.

Converting Text to SmartArt

Sometimes when you are working with text it just doesn't capture your attention, no matter how you dress it up with color or other formatting attributes. The introduction of the SmartArt graphic in PowerPoint 2007 increases your ability to create dynamic-looking text. A **SmartArt** graphic is a professional-quality diagram that visually illustrates text. There are seven basic categories, or types, of SmartArt graphics that illustrate text differently. For example, you can show steps in a process or timeline, show proportional relationships, or show how parts relate to a whole. You can create a SmartArt graphic from scratch or create one by converting existing text you have entered on a slide with a few simple clicks of the mouse. 🎨 At QST, Ellen wants the text to appear visually dynamic so you convert the text on Slide 4 to a SmartArt graphic.

STEPS

1. **On Slide 4, click anywhere in the text object, then click the Convert to SmartArt Graphic button 📊 in the Paragraph group**

   A gallery of SmartArt graphic layouts opens. As with many features in PowerPoint, you can preview how your text will look prior to applying the SmartArt graphic layout by using PowerPoint's Live Preview feature. You can review each SmartArt graphic layout and see how it changes the appearance of text.

2. **Move the pointer over the SmartArt graphic layouts in the gallery**

   Notice how the text becomes part of the graphic and the color and font changes each time you move the pointer over a different graphic layout. SmartArt graphic names appear as ScreenTips.

3. **Click the Basic Timeline layout in the SmartArt graphics gallery**

   A SmartArt graphic appears on the slide in place of the text object and a new SmartArt Tools Design tab opens on the Ribbon as shown in Figure B-5. A SmartArt graphic consists of two parts: the SmartArt graphic itself and a text pane where you type and edit text.

   > **QUICK TIP**
   > The text objects in the SmartArt graphic can be moved and edited like any other text object in PowerPoint.

4. **If necessary, click the Text Pane button in the Create Graphic group to open the text pane, then click each bullet point in the text pane**

   Notice that each time you select a bullet point in the text pane, a selection box appears around the text objects in the SmartArt graphic.

5. **Click the Text Pane button, click the More button ⊽ in the Layouts group, then click the Alternating Flow layout**

   The text pane closes and the SmartArt graphic changes to the new graphic layout. You can radically change how the SmartArt graphic looks by applying a SmartArt Style. A **SmartArt Style** is a pre-set combination of simple and 3-D formatting options that follows the presentation theme.

   > **QUICK TIP**
   > Click the Reset Graphic button in the Reset group to revert the SmartArt graphic to its original state.

6. **Move the pointer slowly over the styles in the SmartArt Styles group, then click the More button ⊽ in the SmartArt Styles group**

   A live preview of each style is displayed on the SmartArt graphic. The SmartArt styles are organized into sections; the top group offers suggestions for the best match for the document.

7. **Move the pointer over the styles in the 3-D section of the gallery, then click Powder**

   Notice how the new Powder style adds a bevel to the text boxes and makes them semi-transparent. Now move the SmartArt graphic more toward the center of the slide.

8. **Press [left-arrow key] twice, click a blank area of the slide outside the SmartArt graphic object to deselect it, then save your work**

   Compare your screen to Figure B-6.

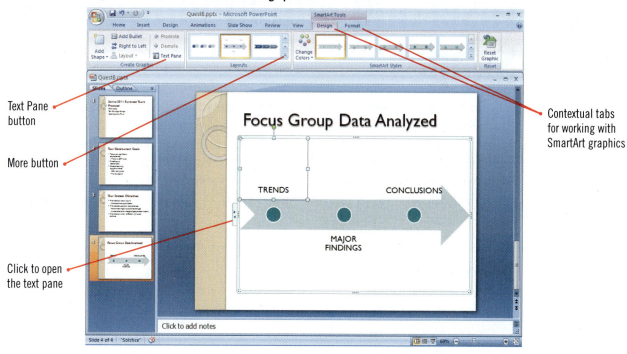

Text Pane button

More button

Click to open the text pane

Contextual tabs for working with SmartArt graphics

FIGURE B-6: Final SmartArt graphic

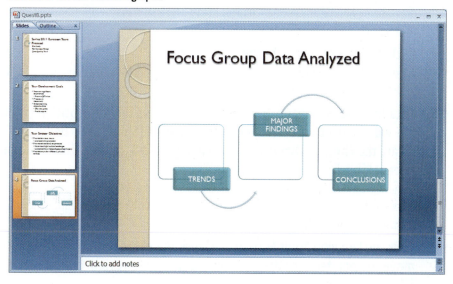

Choosing SmartArt graphics

When choosing a SmartArt graphic to use on your slide, remember that you want the SmartArt graphic to communicate the message of the text effectively; not every SmartArt graphic layout achieves that goal. So, you must consider the type of text you want to illustrate. For example, does the text show steps in a process, does it show a continual process, or does it show non-sequential information? The answer to this question will dictate the type of SmartArt graphic layout you should choose. Also, the amount of text you want to illustrate will have an effect on the SmartArt graphic layout you choose. Most of the time key points will be the text you use in a SmartArt graphic. Finally, some SmartArt graphic layouts are limited by the number of shapes that they can accommodate. So, if you have four points you want to illustrate and you choose a graphic layout with only two shapes, you will not communicate your message correctly. Experiment with the SmartArt graphic layouts until you find the right one, and have fun in the process!

Inserting and Modifying Shapes

In PowerPoint you can insert many different types of shapes including lines, geometric figures, arrows, stars, callouts, and banners to enhance your presentation. You can create single shapes or combine several shapes together to make a more complex figure. You can modify many aspects of a shape including its fill color, line color, and line style, as well as add other effects like shadow, and 3-D effects. Instead of changing individual attributes, you can apply a Quick Style to a shape. A **Quick Style** is a set of formatting options, including line style, fill color, and effects. You decide to draw some shapes on Slide 3 of your presentation to complete the slide.

1. **Click the Slide 3 thumbnail in the Slides tab**

   Slide 3 appears in the Slide pane.

2. **Press and hold [Shift], click the text object, then release [Shift]**

   The text object is selected.

3. **Position the pointer over the bottom-middle sizing handle, notice the pointer change to ↕, then drag the sizing handle up until the text object looks like Figure B-7**

   The text object decreases in size. When you position the pointer over a sizing handle, it changes to ↕. The pointer points in different directions depending on which sizing handle it is positioned over. When you drag a sizing handle, the pointer changes to ＋, and a faint gray outline appears, representing the size of the text object.

TROUBLE

If you see the Shapes gallery on the Ribbon, you are working at a higher resolution than the figures in this book, skip to step 5.

4. **Click the Shapes button in the Drawing group**

   A gallery of shapes organized by type opens. Notice that there is a section at the top of the gallery where all of the recently used shapes are placed.

5. **Click the Chevron shape ▷ in the Block Arrows section, position ＋ in the blank area of the slide below the text object, press and hold [Shift], drag down and to the right to create the chevron shape, as shown in Figure B-8, release the mouse button, then release [Shift]**

   A chevron arrow shape appears on the slide, filled with the default color. Pressing [Shift] while you create the object maintains the object's proportions as you change its size. To change the shape style apply a Quick Style from the Shape Styles group.

TROUBLE

If your shape is not approximately the same size as the one shown in Figure B-8, press [Shift] and drag one of the corner sizing handles to resize the object.

6. **Click the Drawing Tools Format tab, click the More button ▼ in the Shape Styles group, move the pointer over the styles in the gallery to review them, then click Moderate Effect — Accent 3**

   A red Quick Style with coordinated gradient fill, line, and shadow color is applied to the shape.

7. **Click the Shape Effects button in the Shape Styles group, then move the pointer over the effects to review them**

   The shape changes every time you move the pointer over a different effect.

8. **Point to Bevel, click Divot, then save your work**

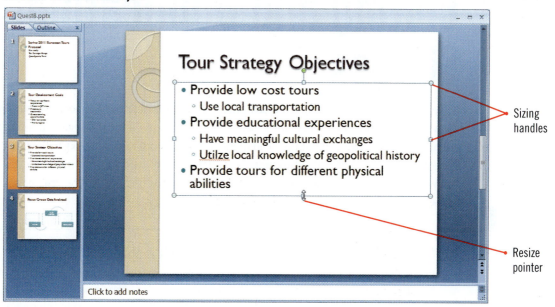

Sizing handles

Resize pointer

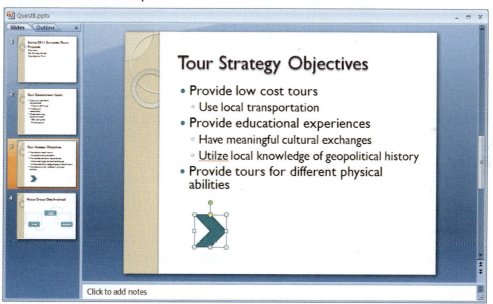

Changing the size and position of shapes

Usually when you resize a shape you can simply drag one of the sizing handles around the outside of the shape, but sometimes you may need to resize a shape more precisely. When you select a shape, the Drawing Tools Format tab appears on the Ribbon, offering you many different formatting options including some sizing commands located in the Size group. The Width and Height commands in the Size group allow you to change the width and height of a shape. You also have the option to open the Size and Position dialog box, which allows you to change the size of a shape, as well as the rotation, scale, and position of a shape on the slide.

Editing and Duplicating Shapes

Once you have created a shape you still have the ability to refine the aspects of the object. PowerPoint allows you to adjust various aspects of shapes to help change the look of them. For example, if you create a shape with an arrowhead but the head of the arrow does not look quite like you want it to look, you can change it. You can also add text to most PowerPoint shapes, and you can move or copy shapes. You want two identical arrows on Slide 3 to break up the look of the slide. You first change the shape of the arrow you've already created, and then you make a copy of it.

STEPS

1. **Click the arrow shape on Slide 3 to select it, if it is not already selected**

   In addition to sizing handles, two other handles appear on the selected object. You use the **adjustment handle**—a small yellow diamond—to change the appearance of an object. The adjustment handle appears next to the most prominent feature of the object, like the head of an arrow in this case. You use the **rotate handle**—a small green circle—to manually rotate the object.

2. **Press and hold [Shift], drag the right-middle sizing handle on the arrow shape to the right approximately 1/2", release [Shift], then release the mouse button**

3. **Position the pointer over the middle of the selected arrow shape so that it changes to ⁺ⁱₖ, then drag the arrow shape so that the arrow aligns with the left edge of the text in the text object as shown in Figure B-9**

   A semitransparent copy of the shape appears as you move the arrow shape to help you position it. PowerPoint uses a hidden grid to align objects; it forces objects to "snap" to the grid lines. Make any needed adjustments to the arrow shape position so it looks similar to Figure B-9.

4. **Position the pointer over the adjustment handle of the arrow shape so that it changes to ▷, then drag the adjustment handle to the right so it is halfway between the sizing handles**

   The arrow shape appearance changes.

5. **Position ⁺ⁱₖ over the arrow shape then press and hold [Ctrl]**

   The pointer changes to ⁺ₖ, indicating that PowerPoint makes a copy of the arrow shape when you drag the mouse.

6. **Holding [Ctrl], drag the arrow shape to the right until the arrow shape copy is in a blank area of the slide, release the mouse button, then release [Ctrl]**

   An identical copy of the arrow shape appears on the slide.

7. **Type Higher**

   The text appears in the selected arrow shape. The text is now part of the shape, so if you move or rotate the object, the text moves with it. Compare your screen with Figure B-10.

8. **Click the other arrow shape, type Aim, then click in a blank area of the slide**

   Clicking a blank area of the slide deselects all objects that are selected.

9. **Save your work**

FIGURE B-9: Slide showing resized shape

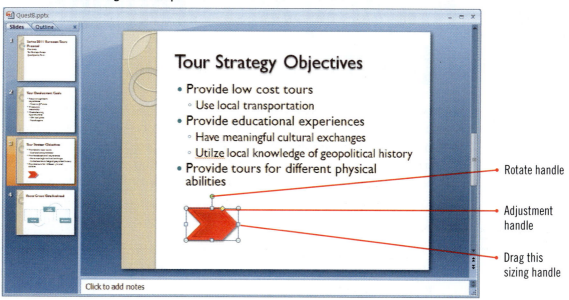

Rotate handle

Adjustment handle

Drag this sizing handle

FIGURE B-10: Slide showing duplicated shape

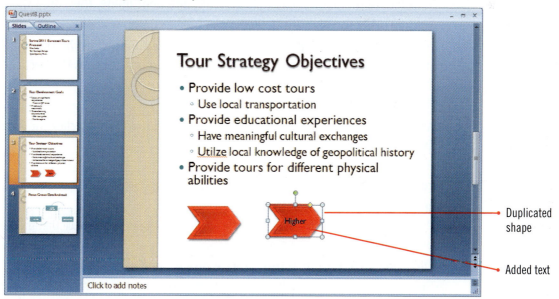

Duplicated shape

Added text

Understanding PowerPoint objects

Every object on a slide, whether it is a text object, a shape, a chart, a picture, or any other object, is stacked on the slide in the order it was created. So, for example, if you add three shapes to a slide, the first shape you create is on the bottom of the stack and the last shape you create is on the top of the stack. Each object, including Title and Content objects, can be moved up or down in the stack depending on how you want the objects to look on the slide. To move an object to the front of the stack, select the object, then click the Bring to Front button in the Arrange group on the Drawing Tools Format tab. To move an object to the back of the stack, click the Send to Back button in the Arrange group on the Drawing Tools Format tab. You can also open the Selection and Visibility pane by clicking the Selection Pane button in the Arrange group to view and rearrange all of the objects on the slide.

Aligning and Grouping Objects

After you are finished creating and modifying your objects, you can position them accurately on the slide to achieve the look you want. Using the Align commands in the Arrange group, you can align objects relative to each other by snapping them to a grid of evenly spaced vertical and horizontal lines. The Group command groups objects into one object, which secures their relative position to each other and makes it easy to edit and move them. The Distribute commands found with the Align commands evenly space objects horizontally or vertically relative to each other or the slide. You are ready to position and group the arrow shapes on Slide 3 to make the slide look consistent and planned.

STEPS

1. **Right-click a blank area of the slide, then click Grid and Guides on the shortcut menu**
   The Grid and Guides dialog box opens.

QUICK TIP

To add a new guide to the slide, press [Ctrl], then drag an existing guide. The original guide remains in place as you move the new guide. Drag a guide off the slide to delete it.

2. **Click the Display drawing guides on screen check box, then click OK**
   The PowerPoint guides appear as dotted lines on the slide and intersect at the center of the slide. They help you position the arrow shape.

3. **Position ☐ over the vertical guide in a blank area of the slide, press and hold the mouse button until the pointer changes to a measurement guide, then drag the guide to the right until the guide position box reads 1.00**

4. **Position ☐ over the Higher arrow shape (not over the text in the shape), then drag the arrow shape so that the left edge of the selection box touches the vertical guide as shown in Figure B-11**
   The arrow shape attaches or "snaps" to the vertical guide.

5. **With the Higher arrow shape selected, press and hold [Shift], click the Aim arrow shape, then release [Shift]**
   The two objects are now selected.

6. **Click the Drawing Tools Format tab on the Ribbon, click the Align button in the Arrange group, then click Align Bottom**
   The objects are now aligned horizontally along their bottom edges. Notice that the Higher arrow shape moves to align with the Aim arrow shape.

7. **Click the Group button in the Arrange group, then click Group**
   The objects group to form one object without losing their individual attributes. Notice that the sizing handles and rotate handle now appear on the outer edge of the grouped object, not around each individual object.

QUICK TIP

Rulers can help you align objects. To display the rulers, position the pointer in a blank area of the slide, right-click, then click Ruler on the shortcut menu.

8. **Click the Align button, click Distribute Horizontally, then click a blank area of the slide**
   The objects are now distributed equally between the edges of the slide. Compare your screen with Figure B-12.

9. **Right-click a blank area of the slide, click Grid and Guides on the shortcut menu, click the Display drawing guides on screen check box, click OK, then save your work**
   The guides are no longer displayed on the slide.

FIGURE B-11: Repositioned shape

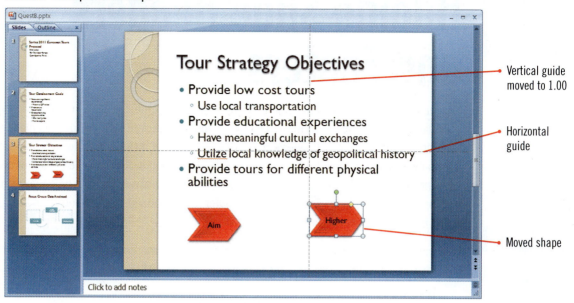

Vertical guide moved to 1.00

Horizontal guide

Moved shape

FIGURE B-12: Aligned and grouped shapes

Distributing objects

There are two ways to distribute objects in PowerPoint: relative to each other and relative to the slide edge. If you choose to distribute objects relative to each other, PowerPoint evenly divides the empty space between all of the selected objects. When distributing objects in relation to the slide, PowerPoint evenly splits the empty space from slide edge to slide edge between the selected objects. To distribute objects relative to each other, click the Align button in the Arrange group on the Format tab, then click Align Selected Objects. To distribute objects relative to the slide, click the Align button in the Arrange group on the Format tab, then click Align to Slide.

Adding Slide Headers and Footers

Header and footer text, such as your company or product name, the slide number, and the date, can give your slides a polished look and make it easier for your audience to follow your presentation. On slides, you can add text to the footer; however, notes or handouts can include both header and footer text. Footer information that you apply to the slides of your presentation is visible in the PowerPoint views and when you print the slides. Notes and handouts header and footer text is visible when you print notes pages, handouts, and the outline. You add footer text to the slides of the European tour proposal presentation to make it easier for the audience to follow.

STEPS

QUICK TIP
The placement of the footer text objects on the slide is dependent upon the presentation theme.

1. **Click the Insert tab on the Ribbon, then click the Header & Footer button in the Text group**

   The Header and Footer dialog box opens, as shown in Figure B-13. The Header and Footer dialog box has two tabs: a Slide tab and a Notes and Handouts tab. The Slide tab is selected. There are three types of footer text, Date and time, Slide number, and Footer. The rectangles at the bottom of the Preview box identify the default position and status of the three types of footer text placeholders on the slides.

2. **Click the Date and time check box to select it**

   The date and time sub-options are now available and the far-left rectangle at the bottom of the Preview box has a dark border around it, signifying where the date and time information will appear on the slide. The Update automatically date and time option button is selected by default. This option updates the date and time every time you open or print the file.

QUICK TIP
If you want a specific date—such as the original date that the presentation was created—to appear every time you view or print the presentation, click the Fixed date option button, then type the date in the Fixed text box.

3. **Click the Update automatically list arrow, then click the fourth option in the list**

   The date format changes to display the month spelled out, the date number, and the four-digit year.

4. **Click the Slide number check box, click the Footer check box, then type Your Name**

   The Preview box now shows that all three footer placeholders are selected.

5. **Click the Don't show on title slide check box**

   Selecting this check box prevents the footer information you entered in the Header and Footer dialog box from appearing on the title slide.

6. **Click Apply to All**

   The dialog box closes and the footer information is applied to all of the slides in your presentation except the title slide. Compare your screen to Figure B-14.

7. **Click the Slide 1 thumbnail in the Slides tab, then click the Header & Footer button in the Text group**

   The Header and Footer dialog box opens again. You want to show your company tag line in the footer on the title slide.

8. **Click the Don't show on title slide check box to deselect it, click the Footer check box, then select the text in the Footer text box**

TROUBLE
If you click Apply to All in Step 9, click the Undo button on the Quick Access toolbar and repeat Steps 7, 8, and 9.

9. **Type "Explore with us...learn from the world", click Apply, then save your work**

   Only the text in the Footer text box appears on the title slide. Clicking Apply applies the footer information to just the current slide.

FIGURE B-13: Header and Footer dialog box

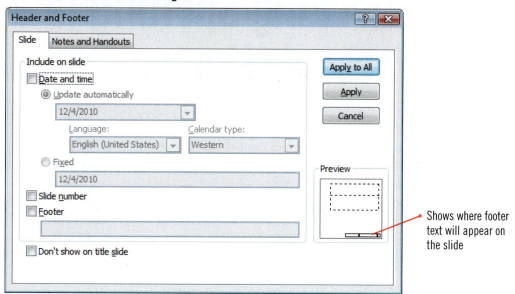

Shows where footer text will appear on the slide

FIGURE B-14: Slide showing footer information

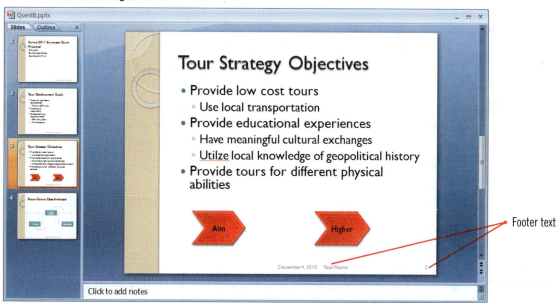

Footer text

Entering and printing notes

You can add notes to your slides when there are certain facts you want to remember during a presentation or when there is information you want to hand out to your audience. Notes do not appear on the slides when you run a slide show. Use the Notes pane in Normal view or Notes Page view to enter notes for your slides. To enter text notes on a slide, click in the Notes pane, then type. If you want to insert graphics as notes, you must use Notes Page view. To open Notes Page view, click the View tab on the Ribbon, then click the Notes Page button in the Presentation Views group. You can print your notes by clicking the Print what list arrow and then clicking Notes Pages in the Print dialog box. The notes page can be a good handout to give your audience to use during the presentation and then after as a reminder. If you don't enter any notes in the Notes pane, and print the notes pages, the slides print as thumbnails with blank lines to the right of the thumbnails to handwrite notes.

Checking Spelling in a Presentation

As your work on the presentation file nears completion, you need to review and proofread your slides thoroughly for errors. You can use the spellchecking feature in PowerPoint to check for and correct spelling errors. This feature compares the spelling of all the words in your presentation against the words contained in PowerPoint's electronic dictionary. You still must proofread your presentation for punctuation, grammar, and word-usage errors because the spellchecker recognizes only misspelled and unknown words, not misused words. For example, the spellchecker would not identify the word "lost" as an error, even if you had intended to type the word "cost."  Ellen wants to present a professional presentation, one without spelling errors. You're finished working with the European tour proposal presentation for now; this is a good time to check the spelling.

STEPS

1. **Click the Review tab on the Ribbon, then click the Spelling button in the Proofing group**

   PowerPoint begins to check the spelling in your presentation. When PowerPoint finds a misspelled word or a word it doesn't recognize, the Spelling dialog box opens, as shown in Figure B-15. In this case, PowerPoint does not recognize the name "Latsky" on Slide 1. It suggests that you replace it with the word "Lastly." You want the word to remain as you typed it.

2. **Click Ignore All**

   Clicking Ignore All tells the spellchecker not to stop at and question any more occurrences of this word in this presentation. The next word the spellchecker identifies as an error is the word "Utilze" in the text object on Slide 3. In the Suggestions list box, the spellchecker suggests "Utilize."

3. **Verify that Utilize is selected in the Suggestions list box, then click Change**

   If PowerPoint finds any other words it does not recognize, either change or ignore them. When the spellchecker finishes checking your presentation, the Spelling dialog box closes, and an alert box opens with a message that the spelling check is complete.

4. **Click OK**

   The alert box closes. You are satisfied with the presentation so far and you decide to print it. Compare your screen to Figure B-16.

5. **Click the Office button, then click the Print button**

   The Print dialog box opens.

6. **Make sure Slides is selected in the Print what list box, then click the Frame slides check box**

   The slides of your presentation print with a frame around each page.

7. **Click OK in the Print dialog box, then save your presentation**

8. **Click the Office button, then click Exit PowerPoint**

FIGURE B-15: Spelling dialog box

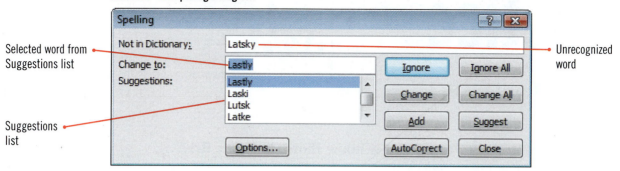

Selected word from Suggestions list

Suggestions list

Unrecognized word

FIGURE B-16: Slide showing fixed spelling error

Fixed spelling error

Checking spelling as you type

PowerPoint checks your spelling as you type. If you type a word that is not in the electronic dictionary, a wavy red line appears under it. To correct an error, right-click the misspelled word, then review the suggestions, which appear in the shortcut menu. You can select a suggestion, add the word you typed to your custom dictionary, or ignore it. To turn off automatic spellchecking, click the Office button, then click the PowerPoint Options button to open the PowerPoint Options dialog box. Click the Proofing button, then click the Check spelling as you type check box to deselect it. To temporarily hide the wavy red lines, click the Hide spelling errors check box to select it.

Practice

If you have a SAM user profile, you may have access to hands-on instruction, practice, and assessment of the skills covered in this unit. Log in to your SAM account (http://sam2007.course.com/) to launch any assigned training activities or exams that relate to the skills covered in this unit.

▼ CONCEPTS REVIEW

Label each element of the PowerPoint window shown in Figure B-17.

FIGURE B-17

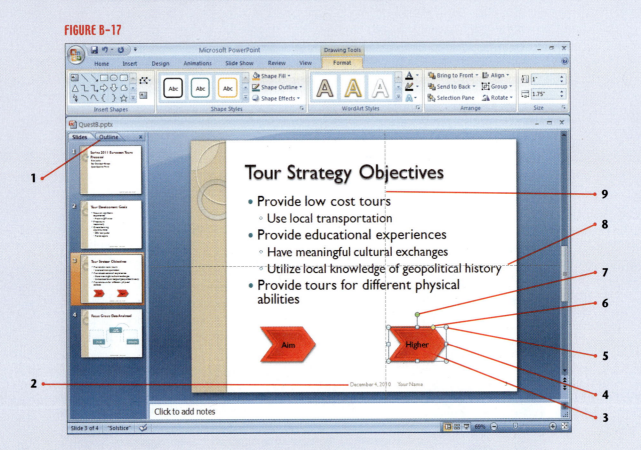

Match each term with the statement that best describes it.

10. Mini toolbar
11. SmartArt graphic
12. Adjustment handle
13. Quick Style
14. Rotate handle
15. Sizing handle

a. A circle or square that appears around a selected object
b. A pre-set combination of formatting options that you apply to an object
c. A formatting toolbar
d. Changes the appearance of an object
e. Allows you to manually rotate an object
f. A diagram that visually illustrates text

Select the best answer from the list of choices.

16. **Which of the following statements about the Mini toolbar is incorrect?**
    a. It is semitransparent until you move the pointer over it.
    b. It is used to change the layout of a slide.
    c. It is used to format text.
    d. It appears when you select text.

17. **Which statement about the PowerPoint spellchecker is true?**
    a. PowerPoint only identifies spelling errors when you run the spellchecker.
    b. The spellchecker catches grammar problems.
    c. The spellchecker identifies misspelled and unknown words.
    d. Most misused words are caught by the spellchecker.

18. **A professional-quality diagram that visually illustrates text best describes which of the following?**
    a. A SmartArt graphic
    b. A shape
    c. A slide layout
    d. A content object

19. **What does the adjustment handle do to a shape?**
    a. Changes the shape to another
    b. Changes the rotation of a shape
    c. Changes the size of a shape
    d. Changes the appearance of a shape

20. **How do you make a shape smaller?**
    a. Drag the adjustment handle.
    b. Drag the sizing handle.
    c. Drag the rotate handle.
    d. Drag the shape edge.

21. **What would you use to place a shape in a specific position on a slide?**
    a. PowerPoint guides
    b. PowerPoint placeholders
    c. PowerPoint distribution angles
    d. PowerPoint anchor points

22. **What is *not* true about grouped objects?**
    a. Grouped objects have one rotate handle.
    b. Sizing handles appear around the grouped object.
    c. Grouped objects lose some of their individual characteristics.
    d. Grouped objects act as one object.

▼ SKILLS REVIEW

1. **Enter text in the Outline tab.**
    a. Open the presentation PPT B-2.pptx from the drive and folder where you store your Data Files, then save it as **TechJet**. The completed presentation is shown in Figure B-18.
    b. Create a new slide after Slide 3 with the Title and Content layout.
    c. Open the Outline tab, then type **Network Integration**.
    d. Press [Enter], press [Tab], type **Protocols and Conversions**, press [Enter], press [Tab], then type **Server codes and routing protocols**.
    e. Press [Enter], type **File transfer**, press [Enter], type **Data conversion**, press [Enter], then type **Platform functionality ratings**.
    f. Move Slide 4 to the Slide 3 position.

FIGURE B-18

    g. Switch back to the Slides tab.

    h. Save your changes.

2. Format text.

    a. Go to Slide 1.

    b. Select the name Joseph M. Sera, then move the pointer over the Mini toolbar.

    c. Click the Font Color list arrow, then click Orange under Standard Colors.

    d. Using [Shift] select the text object, then change all of the text to the color Orange.

    e. Click the Font Size list arrow, then click 24.

    f. Click the Bold button.

    g. Save your changes.

3. Convert text to SmartArt.

    a. Click the text object on Slide 4.

    b. Apply the Basic Cycle SmartArt graphic layout to the text object.

    c. Click the More button in the SmartArt Styles group, then apply the Inset style to the graphic.

    d. Reposition the diagram to the center of the slide, if necessary.

    e. Click outside the SmartArt graphic in an empty part of the slide.

    f. Save your changes.

4. Insert and modify shapes.

    a. Go to Slide 3.

FIGURE B-19

    b. Using [Shift] select the text object, then drag the bottom-middle sizing handle up to decrease the size of the text object.

    c. Click the Insert tab on the Ribbon, then insert the Left-Right-Up Arrow shape from the Shapes gallery similar to the one in Figure B-19.

    d. Type **Routing protocols**, then click Moderate Effect – Accent 3 in the Shape Styles group.

    e. Click the Shape Effects button in the Shape Styles group, point to Shadow, then click Offset Bottom.

    f. Click the Shape Fill button in the Shape Styles group, point to Gradient, then click Linear Up.

    g. Click a blank area of the slide, then save your changes.

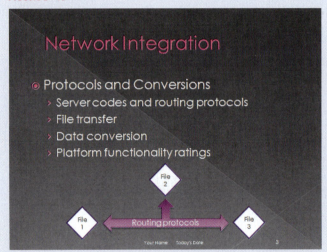

5. Edit and duplicate shapes.

    a. Insert a Diamond shape from the Shapes gallery to the left of the arrow shape.

    b. Click the More button in the Shape Styles group, click Colored Outline – Accent 4, then type **File 1**.

    c. Drag to select the text File 1, click the Home tab, click the Font Size button in the Font group, then click 14.

    d. Using [Ctrl] make two copies of the diamond shape, then change the text in one shape to **File 2** and the text in the other shape to **File 3**.

    e. Move the File 2 diamond shape to the top of the arrow shape and the File 3 diamond shape to the right of the arrow shape, as shown in Figure B-19.

    f. Click a blank area of the slide, then save your changes.

6. Align and group objects.

    a. Hold down [Shift], click the File 1 diamond shape, click the File 3 diamond shape, then release [Shift].

    b. Click the Drawing Tools Format tab if necessary, click Align, click Align Middle.

    c. Hold down [Shift], click the arrow shape, click the File 2 diamond shape, click the Group button in the Arrange group, then click Group.

    d. Click the Align button in the Arrange group, then click Distribute Horizontally.

    e. Save your work.

7. **Add slide headers and footers.**

   a. Open the Header and Footer dialog box.

   b. In the Slide tab, type today's date into the Fixed text box.

   c. Add the slide number to the footer.

   d. Type your name in the Footer text box.

   e. Apply the footer to all of the slides except the title slide.

   f. Open the Header and Footer dialog box again, then click the Notes and Handouts tab.

   g. Enter today's date in the Fixed text box.

   h. Type the name of your class in the Header text box, then click the Page number check box.

   i. Type your name in the Footer text box.

   j. Apply the header and footer information to all the notes and handouts.

   k. Save your changes.

8. **Check spelling in a presentation.**

   a. Perform a spelling check on the document and change any misspelled words. Ignore any words that are correctly spelled but that the spellchecker doesn't recognize. There is at least one misspelled word in the presentation.

   b. Save your changes, then close the file and exit PowerPoint.

▼ INDEPENDENT CHALLENGE 1

You are the Director of the Westminster Theater Arts Center in Kansas City, Missouri, and one of your many duties is to raise funds to cover operation costs. One of the primary ways you do this is by speaking to businesses, community clubs, and other organizations throughout the Kansas City region. Every year you speak to many organizations, where you give a short presentation detailing what the theater center plans to do for the coming season. You need to continue working on the presentation you started already.

a. Start PowerPoint, open the presentation PPT B-3.pptx from the drive and folder where you store your Data Files, and save it as **WTAC 2011**.

b. Use the Outline tab to enter the following as bulleted text on the Commitment to Excellence slide:

Study

Diligence

Testing

Excellence

c. Apply the Verve design theme to the presentation.

d. Change the font color of each play name on Slide 3 to Yellow.

e. Change the bulleted text on Slide 5 to the Basic Cycle SmartArt graphic layout, then apply the Polished SmartArt Style.

Advanced Challenge Exercise

■ Open the Notes Page view.

■ To at least two slides, add notes that relate to the slide content that you think would be important when giving this presentation.

■ Save the presentation as **WTAC 2011 ACE** to the drive and folder where you store your Data Files, then print the Notes Page view for the presentation.

f. Check the spelling in the presentation then view the presentation in Slide Show view.

g. Add your name as a footer on the notes and handouts, print handouts (three slides per page), and then print the presentation outline.

h. Save your changes, close your presentation, then exit PowerPoint.

▼ INDEPENDENT CHALLENGE 2

You are a manager for Schweizerhaus, Ltd., a Swiss mortgage loan company headquartered in Bern, Switzerland. You have been asked by your boss to develop a presentation outlining important details and aspects of the mortgage process for clients and investors. The focus of the presentation is the use of mortgage brokers to secure loans for clients.

a. Start PowerPoint, open the presentation PPT B-4.pptx from the drive and folder where you store your Data Files, and save it as **Loan Broker**.

b. Apply the Technic design theme to the presentation.

c. On Slide 4 select the three shapes, Banks, Mortgage Bankers, and Private Investors, then using the Align command distribute them vertically and align them to their left edges.

d. On Slide 4 select the three shapes, Borrower, Mortgage Broker, and Mortgage Bankers, then using the Align command distribute them horizontally and align them to their bottom edges.

e. Select all of the shapes, then apply Moderate Effect – Accent 2 from the Shape Styles group.

f. Using the Arrow shape from the Shapes gallery, draw a 3pt arrow between all of the shapes as shown in Figure B-20. (*Hint*: Draw one arrow shape, change the line weight to 3 pt using the Shape Outline button, then duplicate the shape.)

g. Create a sixth slide to end the presentation with the following information:
Schweizerhaus, Ltd.
Zieglerstrasse 765, Bern
TEL: 3937095, FAX: 9375719

h. Check the spelling in the presentation, view the presentation in Slide Show view, then view the slides in Slide Sorter view.

i. Add your name as a footer on the notes and handouts, print the presentation as handouts (two slides per page), then print the presentation outline.

j. Save your changes, close your presentation, then exit PowerPoint.

FIGURE B-20

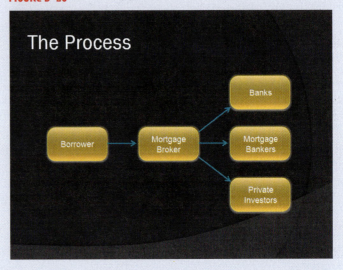

▼ INDEPENDENT CHALLENGE 3

You are an independent distributor of natural foods in Bellingham, Washington. Your business, NorthWest Natural Foods, has grown progressively since its inception five years ago, but sales and profits have leveled off over the last nine months. In an effort to stimulate growth, you decide to acquire All Natural Inc., a major natural food dealer in California, which would allow your company to begin expanding into surrounding states. Use PowerPoint to develop a presentation that you can use to gain a financial backer for the acquisition. Create your own information for the presentation.

a. Start PowerPoint, create a new presentation, then apply the Concourse design theme to the presentation.

b. Enter **A Plan for Growth** as the main title on the title slide, and **NorthWest Natural Foods** as the subtitle.

c. Save the presentation as **NW Natural** to the drive and folder where you store your Data Files.

d. Add five more slides with the following titles: Slide 2-Background; Slide 3-Current Situation; Slide 4-Acquisition Goals; Slide 5-Our Management Team; Slide 6-Funding Required.

e. Enter text into the text placeholders of the slides. Use both the Slide pane and the Outline tab to enter text.

f. Convert text on one slide to a SmartArt graphic, then apply the SmartArt graphic style Subtle Effect.

▼ INDEPENDENT CHALLENGE 3 (CONTINUED)

Advanced Challenge Exercise

- ■ Click the Replace button arrow in the Editing group on the Home tab, then click Replace Fonts.
- ■ Replace the Eras Medium ITC font with the Arial font.
- ■ Save the presentation as **NW Natural ACE** to the drive and folder where you store your Data Files.

g. Check the spelling in the presentation, view the presentation as a slide show, then view the slides in Slide Sorter view.

h. Add your name as a footer on the slides, save your changes, then print the slides.

i. Close your presentation, then exit PowerPoint.

▼ REAL LIFE INDEPENDENT CHALLENGE

Your computer professor at Central State University has been asked by the department head to convert his Applied Technology course into an accelerated course that both students and professional working people can take. Your professor has asked you to help him create a presentation for the class that he can post on the Internet and use as a promotional tool at local businesses. Most of the raw information is already on the slides, you primarily need to jazz it up by adding a theme, and some text formatting.

a. Start PowerPoint, open the presentation PPT B-5.pptx from drive and folder where you store your data files, and save it as **Applied Tech**.

b. Add a new slide after the Course Facts slide with the same layout, type **Course Details** in the title text placeholder, then enter the following as bulleted text in the Outline tab:

Unix/Information Systems
Networking
Applied Methods
Technology Solutions
Software Design
Applications

c. Apply the Origin theme to the presentation.

d. Select the title text object on Slide 1 (*Hint*: Press [Shift] to select the whole object), then change the text color to Dark Red.

e. Change the font of the title text object to Bernard MT Condensed.

f. Change the text on Slide 4 to a SmartArt graphic. The text on this slide is a list so make sure the diagram type you choose is appropriate for the text.

g. Change the style of the SmartArt diagram using one of the SmartArt Styles, then view the presentation in Slide Show view.

h. Add the slide number and your name as a footer on the notes and handouts, print handouts (four slides per page), and then print the presentation outline.

i. Save your changes, close your presentation, then exit PowerPoint.

▼ VISUAL WORKSHOP

Create the presentation shown in Figures B-21 and B-22. Add today's date as the date on the title slide. Save the presentation as **Trade Analysis** to the drive and folder where you store your Data Files. Review your slides in Slide Show view, then add your name as a footer to the notes and handouts. Print the slides of your presentation, then print the outline. Save your changes, close the presentation, then exit PowerPoint.

FIGURE B-21

FIGURE B-22

Inserting Objects into a Presentation

A good presenter will make use of visual elements, such as charts, graphics, and photographs, in conjunction with text to help communicate the presentation message. Visual elements keep the presentation interesting and help the audience focus on what the presenter is saying. In this unit, you continue working on the presentation for your boss Ellen Latsky by inserting visual elements, including clip art, a picture, and a chart, into the presentation. You format these objects using PowerPoint's powerful object editing features.

OBJECTIVES

Insert text from Microsoft Word

Insert clip art

Insert and style a picture

Insert a text box

Insert a chart

Enter and edit chart data

Insert a table

Insert and format WordArt

Inserting Text from Microsoft Word

PowerPoint makes it easy to insert text from other sources into a presentation. Documents saved in Microsoft Word format (.docx), Rich Text Format (.rtf), plain text format (.txt), and HTML format (.htm) can be inserted into a presentation. If you have an existing Word document or outline, you can import it into PowerPoint to create a new presentation or use it to insert additional slides in an existing presentation. When you import a Microsoft Word or a Rich Text Format document into a presentation, PowerPoint creates an outline structure based on the styles in the document. For example, a Heading 1 style in the Word document becomes a slide title in PowerPoint and a Heading 2 style becomes the first level of text in a bulleted list. If you insert a plain text format document into a presentation, PowerPoint creates an outline based on the tabs at the beginning of the document's paragraphs. Paragraphs without tabs become slide titles; paragraphs with one tab indent become first-level text in bulleted lists; paragraphs with two tabs become second-level text in bulleted lists; and so on. Ron Dawson, QST's Vice President of Marketing, sent you a Microsoft Word document with data from a focus group study QST held last spring. You use this information in the presentation.

STEPS

1. **Start PowerPoint, open the presentation PPT C-1.pptx from the drive and folder where you store your Data Files, save it as QuestC, click the View tab on the Ribbon, then click the Arrange All button in the Window group**

2. **Click the Outline tab, then click the Slide 4 icon in the Outline tab**
   Slide 4 appears in the Slide pane. Each time you click a slide icon in the Outline tab, the slide title and text are highlighted indicating the slide is selected. Before you insert information into a presentation, you must first designate where you want the information to be placed. In this case, the Word document will be inserted after Slide 4, the selected slide.

3. **Click the Home tab on the Ribbon, click the New Slide button list arrow in the Slides group, then click Slides from Outline**
   The Insert Outline dialog box opens.

4. **Select the Word document file PPT C-2.docx from the drive and folder where you store your Data Files, then click Insert**
   Four new slides (5, 6, 7, and 8) are added to the presentation. See Figure C-1.

5. **Read the text for the new Slide 5 in the Slide pane, then review the text on slides 6, 7, and 8 in the Outline tab**
   After reviewing the text on the new slides, you realize that the information on Slide 8 is not necessary for the presentation.

6. **Click the Slides tab, then right-click the Slide 8 thumbnail**
   A shortcut menu opens displaying a number of common commands. Right-clicking most objects in PowerPoint opens a shortcut menu.

7. **Click Delete Slide on the shortcut menu**
   Slide 8 is deleted from the presentation. The last slide in the presentation displaying a picture placeholder now appears in the Slide pane. You also notice that Slide 6 should come before Slide 5.

8. **Click Slide 6 in the Slides tab, then drag it above Slide 5**
   Slide 6 and Slide 5 change places. Compare your screen to Figure C-2.

9. **Click the Save button on the Quick Access Toolbar**

FIGURE C-1: Outline tab showing imported text

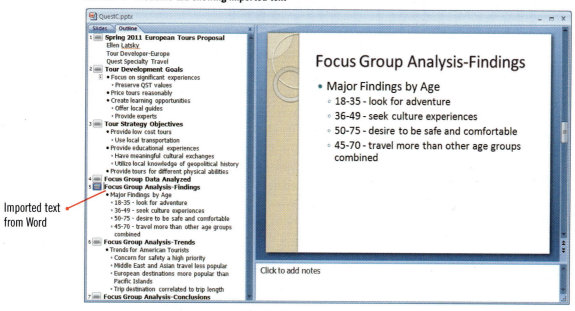

Imported text from Word

FIGURE C-2: Presentation after moving a slide

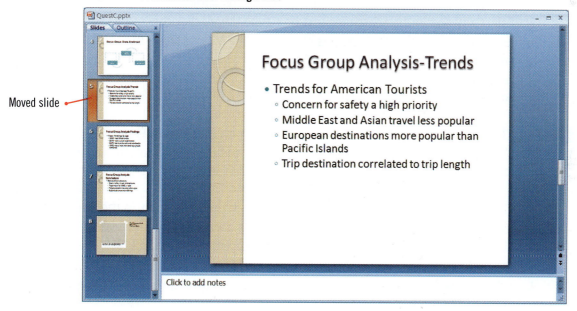

Moved slide

Inserting slides from other presentations

To insert slides from another presentation into the current presentation, click the New Slide button list arrow in the Slides group, then click Reuse Slides. The Reuse Slides task pane opens on the right side of the window. Click the Open a PowerPoint File link, locate the presentation you want to use, then click Open. Click the slide(s) to place them in the presentation. The new slides automatically take on the theme of the current presentation. You can also copy slides from one presentation to another. Open both presentations, change the view of each presentation to Slide Sorter view or use the Arrange All command to see both presentations, select the desired slides, then copy and paste them (or use drag and drop) into the desired presentation.

Inserting Clip Art

PowerPoint has access to many professionally designed graphics, called **clip art**, which you can place in your presentation. In Microsoft Office, clip art and other media files, including photographs, movies, and sounds, are stored in a file index system called the Microsoft Clip Organizer and are identified by descriptive keywords. The Clip Organizer sorts the clip art into groups, including My Collections, Office Collections, and Web Collections. The Office Collections group holds all the media files that come with Microsoft Office. You can customize the Clip Organizer by adding clips to a collection, moving clips from one collection to another, or creating a new collection. As with drawn objects, you can modify clip art images by changing their shape, size, fill, or shading. Clip art is available from many sources outside the Clip Organizer, including the Microsoft Office Online Web site and commercially available collections that you can purchase. To enhance the QST presentation, you add a clip from the Clip Organizer to one of the slides and then adjust its size and placement.

STEPS

1. **Click the up scroll arrow in the Slides tab until Slide 2 appears, click the Slide 2 thumbnail, then click the Clip Art icon in the Content placeholder**

   The Clip Art task pane opens. At the top of the task pane in the Search for text box, you enter a keyword to search for clips that meet that description. You can search for a clip in a specific collection or in all collections. You can also search for a clip that is a specific media type, such as clip art, photographs, movies, or sounds. At the bottom of the task pane, you can click a hyperlink to organize clips, locate other pieces of clip art at the Office Online Web site, or read tips on how to find clip art.

2. **Select any text in the Search for text box, type travel, click the Results should be list arrow, then click the Photographs check box, the Movies check box, and the Sounds check box to remove the check marks**

   Since you are only interested in finding clip art, deselecting the Photographs, Movies, and Sounds check boxes significantly reduces the amount of media PowerPoint needs to search through to produce your results. PowerPoint searches for clips identified by the keyword "travel."

   > **QUICK TIP**
   > If an alert dialog box appears asking if you want to add additional images from Microsoft Office Online, click Yes

3. **Click the Go button, then click the clip art thumbnail shown in Figure C-3**

   The clip art object appears in the content placeholder and the Picture Tools Format tab appears on the Ribbon. If you don't see the clip shown in Figure C-3, select another one. Although you can change a clip's size by dragging a corner sizing handle, you can also **scale** it to change its size by a specific percentage.

4. **Click the Size and Position dialog box launcher in the Size group, in the Scale section make sure the Lock aspect ratio check box has a check mark, in the Scale section click the Height up arrow until the Height and Width percentages display 110%, then click Close**

   The clip proportionally increases in size.

5. **Click the Picture Border button in the Picture Styles group, then click the Aqua, Accent 1 color box in the top row**

   A light blue border appears around the object.

   > **QUICK TIP**
   > You can use the Reset Picture button in the Adjust group to reset the object formatting.

6. **Click the Picture Border button, point to Weight, then click the 3 pt solid line style**

   The clip now has a 3-point solid border. It appears to be framed.

7. **Drag the clip art object straight down even with the bottom line of text**

   You don't like the new placement of the clip.

8. **Click the Undo button on the Quick Access toolbar, click a blank area of the slide, then save your changes**

9. **Click the Results should be list arrow in the Clip Art task pane, click the All media types check box, click Go, then click the task pane Close button**

   Now the next time you search for a clip, PowerPoint will search through all media types. Compare the slide on your screen to the slide shown in Figure C-4.

FIGURE C-3: Screen showing Clip Art task pane

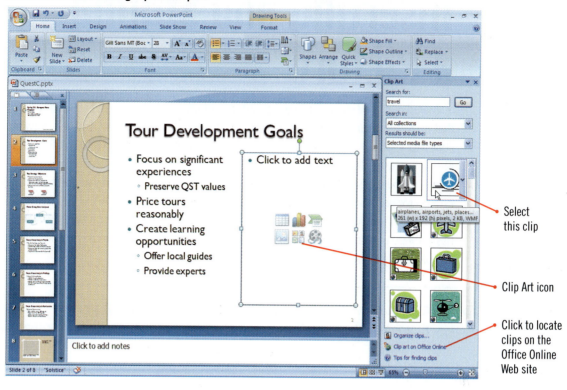

Select this clip

Clip Art icon

Click to locate clips on the Office Online Web site

FIGURE C-4: Slide with formatted clip art object

3pt solid frame

Finding more clips online

If you can't find exactly what you want in the Clip Organizer, you can easily download and use clips from the Clip Art and Media Web page in the Microsoft Office Online Web site. To get clips from the Clip Art Web page, click the Clip art on Office Online hyperlink at the bottom of the Clip Art task pane. If your computer is connected to the Internet, this will launch your Web browser and automatically connect you to the Microsoft Office Online Web site. You can search the site by keyword or browse by media type category. Each clip you download is automatically inserted into the Clip Organizer Web Collections folder and appears in the Clip Art task pane.

Inserting and Styling a Picture

In PowerPoint, a **picture** is defined as a digital photograph, a piece of line art or clip art, or other artwork that is created in another program and inserted into a PowerPoint presentation. PowerPoint gives you the ability to insert 17 different types of pictures including JPEG File Interchange Format and BMP Windows Bitmap. As with all objects in PowerPoint, you can format and style inserted pictures to help them fit the theme of your presentation. You can also hide a portion of the picture you don't want visible by **cropping** it. The cropped portion of a picture, unlike other objects such as clip art, is automatically deleted when the presentation is saved unless you change the setting in the Compression Settings dialog box. 🎨 QST has a library of pictures from tours available to use in presentations. In this lesson, you insert a picture that has previously been saved to a file, and then you crop it and style it.

STEPS

QUICK TIP

You can also insert a picture by clicking the Picture button in the Illustrations group on the Insert tab.

1. **Click the down scroll arrow in the Slides tab until Slide 8 appears, click the Slide 8 thumbnail, then click the Insert Picture from File icon 🖼 in the content placeholder on the slide**

   The Insert Picture dialog box opens displaying the pictures available in the Pictures folder. The Pictures folder is the default folder.

2. **Select the picture file PPT C-3.jpg from the drive and folder where you store your Data Files, then click Insert**

   The picture appears in the Picture placeholder on the slide and the Picture Tools Format tab opens on the Ribbon. The picture would look better if you cropped some of the beach off the bottom.

3. **Click the Crop button in the Size group, then place the pointer over the bottom-middle sizing handle of the picture**

   The pointer changes to **⊤**. When the Crop button is active, the sizing handles appear as straight black lines.

4. **Press and hold [Alt], drag the bottom edge of the picture up until the lower-left corner of the picture is at the water line as shown in Figure C-5, then click the Crop button**

   Pressing [Alt] while dragging or drawing an object in PowerPoint overrides the automatic snap-to-grid setting. PowerPoint has a number of picture formatting options, and you decide to experiment with some of them.

5. **Click the Picture Styles More button 🔻, then click Bevel Rectangle (3rd row)**

   The picture changes shape. Notice that this particular style includes an adjustment handle so that you can adjust the shape of the picture.

6. **Click the Recolor button in the Adjust group, click Sepia in the Color Modes section, then click the Slide Show button 🖵 in the status bar**

   The slide fills your screen. After evaluating the slide you conclude that the shape and color changes you've made to the picture don't improve the look of the slide.

7. **Press [Esc], click the Undo button list arrow on the Quick Access toolbar, then click Format Picture**

   All of the formatting changes you made to the picture are removed. The cropped portion of the picture does not change and remains hidden.

8. **Click the Picture Styles More button, click Drop Shadow Rectangle (1st row), click a blank area on the slide, then save your changes**

   Compare your screen to Figure C-6.

FIGURE C-5: Using the cropping pointer to crop a picture

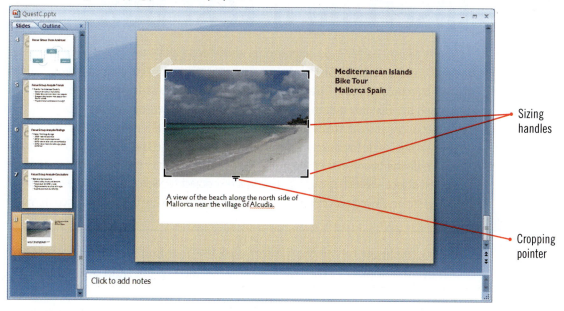

Sizing handles

Cropping pointer

FIGURE C-6: Cropped and styled picture

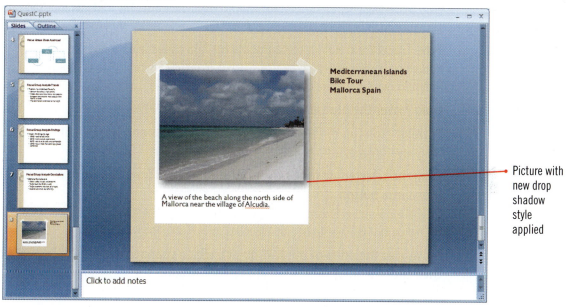

Picture with new drop shadow style applied

Picture compression

By default, all inserted pictures in PowerPoint 2007 are automatically compressed every time you save your presentation. If you want to prohibit the automatic compression of pictures or be able to choose individual pictures to compress, select a picture, then click the Picture Tools Format tab. Click the Compress Pictures button in the Adjust group, then click Options in the Compress Pictures dialog box. The Compression Settings dialog box opens. Notice that PowerPoint compresses pictures every time the presentation is saved and deletes cropped portions of pictures to save space. To compress individual pictures, make sure the top option in the Compression Settings dialog box is deselected, select a picture, click the Compress Pictures button, then click OK. To stop PowerPoint from automatically deleting cropped portions of pictures, deselect the check box next to the Delete cropped areas of pictures option in the Compression Settings dialog box.

UNIT C

PowerPoint 2007

Inserting a Text Box

As you've already learned, you enter text on a slide using a title or content placeholder that is arranged on the slide based on a particular slide layout. Every so often you need additional text on a slide where the traditional placeholder does not place text effectively for your message. You can create an individual text object by clicking the Text Box button in the Text group on the Insert tab on the Ribbon. There are two types of text objects that you can create: a text label, used for a small phrase where text doesn't automatically wrap to the next line inside the box; and a word processing box, used for a sentence or paragraph where the text wraps inside the boundaries of the box. Either type of text box can be formatted and edited just like any other text object. You decide to add a text object to Slide 8 to finish the information about the bike tour. You create a word processing box on the slide, enter text, edit text, and then format the text.

STEPS

1. **Click the Insert tab on the Ribbon, click the Text Box button in the Text group, then move the pointer to the blank area of the slide to the right of the picture**
   The pointer changes to ↓.

QUICK TIP

To create a text label in which text doesn't wrap, click the Text Box button, position ↓ where you want to place the text, click once, then enter your text.

2. **Drag down and toward the right side of the slide about an inch and a half to create a word processing box**
   When you begin dragging, an outline of the text object appears, indicating how large a text object you are drawing. After you release the mouse button, an insertion point appears inside the text object, in this case a word processing box, which indicates that you can enter text. The font and font style appear in the Font group on the Ribbon.
3. **Type Travel from Palma to La Puebla for 135 miles over 6 days**
   Notice that the text object increases in size as your text wraps inside the text object. Your screen should look similar to Figure C-7. After entering the text you realize there is a mistake.
4. **Drag I over the phrase for 135 miles to select it**
5. **Position ↖ on top of the selected phrase and press and hold the mouse button**
   The pointer changes to ↖.

QUICK TIP

You can also move text between text objects on a slide and in the Outline tab using this drag-and-drop method.

6. **Drag the selected words to the right of the word Travel in the text object, then release the mouse button**
   A light blue insertion line appears as you drag, indicating where PowerPoint places the text when you release the mouse button. The phrase "for 135 miles" moves after the word "Travel".
7. **Move ↖ to the edge of the text object, which changes to ✥, click the text object border, then click the Italic button I in the Font group**
   All of the text in the text object is italicized.
8. **Drag the right-middle sizing handle of the text object to the right until the text is on two lines, position ✥ over the text object edge, then drag it next to the picture caption**
   Your screen should look similar to Figure C-8.
9. **Click a blank area of the slide outside the text object, then save your changes**

FIGURE C-7: New text object

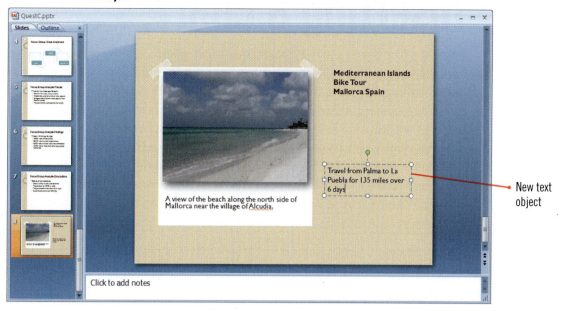

New text object

FIGURE C-8: Formatted text object

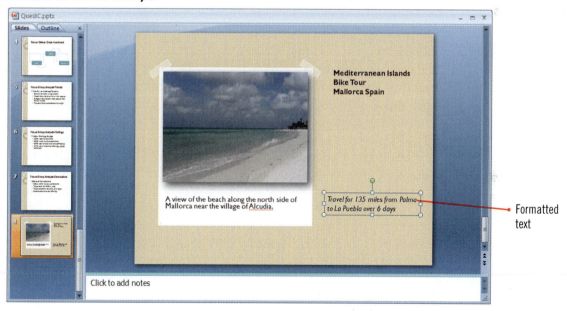

Formatted text

Sending a presentation using e-mail

You can send a copy of a presentation over the Internet to a reviewer for them to edit and add comments. You can use Microsoft Outlook, or any other compatible e-mail program, to send your presentation. Although your e-mail program allows you to attach files, you can send a presentation using Outlook from within PowerPoint. Click the Office button, point to Send, then click Email. Outlook opens and automatically creates an e-mail with the presentation attached to it. The recipient of the presentation can use PowerPoint 2007 or an earlier version of PowerPoint to edit the presentation or add comments. To open a PowerPoint 2007 file in an earlier version of PowerPoint, you must save the presentation as a PowerPoint 97-2003 presentation or install the Compatibility Pack for the Office 2007 Office system files from Microsoft's Web site. Once the presentation is back in your hands, you can view, edit, or delete the reviewer's comments.

Inserting a Chart

Often, the best way to communicate numerical information is with a visual aid such as a chart. If you have Microsoft Excel installed on your computer, PowerPoint uses Excel to create charts. If you don't have Excel installed, a charting program called **Microsoft Graph** opens that you can use to create charts for your slides. A **chart** is the graphical representation of numerical data. Every chart has a corresponding **worksheet** that contains the numerical data displayed by the chart. When you insert a chart object into PowerPoint, you are actually embedding it. An **embedded** object is one that is a part of your presentation (just like any other object you insert into PowerPoint) except that an embedded object's data source can be opened, in this case Excel, for editing purposes. Changes you make to an embedded object in PowerPoint using PowerPoint's features do not affect the data source for the data. You insert a chart on a new slide that graphically shows results from an online survey Ellen Latsky conducted.

STEPS

1. **Verify that Slide 8 is selected, click the New Slide button list arrow in the Slides group, then click Title and Content**

   A new slide is added to your presentation with the Title and Content slide layout.

2. **Click the Insert Chart icon 📊 in the Content placeholder**

   The Insert Chart dialog box opens as shown in Figure C-9. Each chart type includes a number of 2-D and 3-D styles. The Column chart type, for example, includes 19 different styles and the Line chart type includes 7 different styles. The Clustered Column chart is the default chart style. For a brief explanation of how each of these chart types graphs data, refer to Table C-1.

3. **Click OK**

   Excel opens in a split window sharing the computer screen with the PowerPoint window as shown in Figure C-10. The PowerPoint window displays the clustered column chart and the Excel window displays sample data in a worksheet. The Chart Tools Design tab on the Ribbon contains commands you use in PowerPoint to work with the chart. The worksheet consists of rows and columns. The intersection of a row and a column is called a **cell**. Cells are referred to by their row and column location; for example, the cell at the intersection of column A and row 1 is called cell A1. Cells in the first or left column contain **axis labels** that identify the data in a row for example, "Category 1" is an axis label. Cells in the first or top row are **legend** names and provide further information about the data. Cells below and to the right of the axis labels and legend names contain the data values that are represented in the chart. Each column and row of data in the worksheet is called a **data series**. Each data series has corresponding **data series markers** in the chart, which are graphical representations such as bars, columns, or pie wedges. The gray boxes with the numbers along the left side of the worksheet are called **row headings**, and the gray boxes with the letters along the top of the worksheet are called **column headings**.

4. **Move the pointer over the worksheet in the Excel window**

   The pointer changes to ✛. Cell A6 is the **active cell**, which means that it is selected. The active cell has a thick black border around it.

5. **Click cell C4**

   Cell C4 is now the active cell.

6. **Click the Excel Window Close button ⊠ on the title bar**

   The Excel window closes and the PowerPoint window fills the screen. A new chart object appears on the slide displaying the data from the Excel worksheet.

7. **Click in a blank area of the slide to deselect the chart object**

   The Chart Tools Design Ribbon is no longer active.

8. **Click the slide Title placeholder, type On-line Survey Results, then save your changes**

FIGURE C-9: Insert Chart dialog box

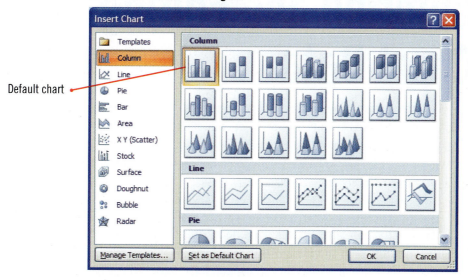

Default chart

FIGURE C-10: The PowerPoint and Excel split windows

Chart Tools
Design tab
on the
Ribbon

Inserted
chart in
PowerPoint

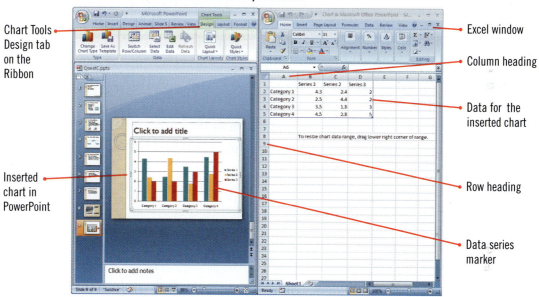

Excel window

Column heading

Data for the
inserted chart

Row heading

Data series
marker

TABLE C-1: Chart types

chart type	icon looks like	use to
Column		Track values over time or across categories
Line		Track values over time
Pie		Compare individual values to the whole
Bar		Compare values in categories or over time
Area		Show contribution of each data series to the total over time
XY (Scatter)		Compare pairs of values
Stock		Show stock market information or scientific data
Surface		Show value trends across two dimensions
Doughnut		Compare individual values to the whole with multiple series
Bubble		Indicate relative size of data points
Radar		Show changes in values in relation to a center point

Entering and Editing Chart Data

After you insert a chart into your presentation, you need to replace the sample data with the correct information. If you have data in an Excel worksheet or another source, you can import it into Excel; otherwise you can type your own information into the worksheet. As you enter data and make other changes in the Excel worksheet, the chart in PowerPoint automatically reflects the new changes.  You enter and format the survey data collected by Ellen.

1. **Click the chart on Slide 9, click the Chart Tools Design tab on the Ribbon, then click the Edit Data button in the Data group**

   The chart is selected in PowerPoint and the worksheet opens in a separate Excel window. The data in the worksheet needs to be replaced with the correct information.

2. **Click the Series 1 cell, type Safety, press [Tab], type Price, press [Tab], then type Experience**

   The Legend labels are entered. Pressing [Tab] in Excel moves the active cell from left to right one cell at a time in a row. Pressing [Enter] in the worksheet moves the active cell down one cell at a time in a column.

3. **Click the Category 1 cell, type 2 Years Past, press [Enter], type Last Year, press [Enter], then type This Year**

   The axis labels are entered and the chart in the PowerPoint window reflects all the changes.

4. **Enter the remainder of the data shown in Figure C-11 to complete the worksheet, then press [Enter]**

   The sample information in Row 5 of the worksheet is not needed.

5. **Right-click the Row 5 row heading, then click Delete**

   Clicking a row heading selects the entire row. The chart currently shows the rows grouped by year, and the legend represents the columns in the datasheet. It would be more effective if the row data appeared in the legend so you could compare yearly results.

6. **Click the Switch Row/Column button in the Data group in the PowerPoint window**

   You have finished entering data in the Excel worksheet.

7. **Click the Excel window Close button** ☒

   Notice that the height of each column in the chart, as well as the values along the vertical axis, adjust to reflect the numbers you typed. The vertical axis is also called the **Value axis**. The horizontal axis is called the **Category axis**. The column labels are now on the Category axis of the chart, and the row labels are listed in the legend.

8. **Click a blank area on the slide, then save the presentation**

   Compare your chart to Figure C-12.

FIGURE C-11: Worksheet showing chart data

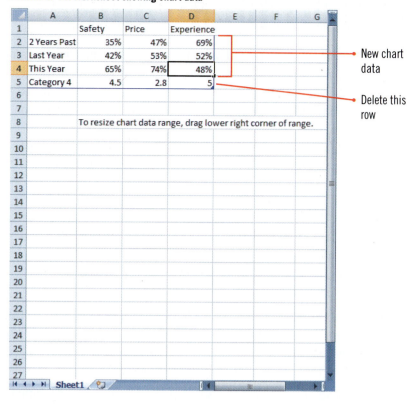

New chart data

Delete this row

FIGURE C-12: Formatted chart

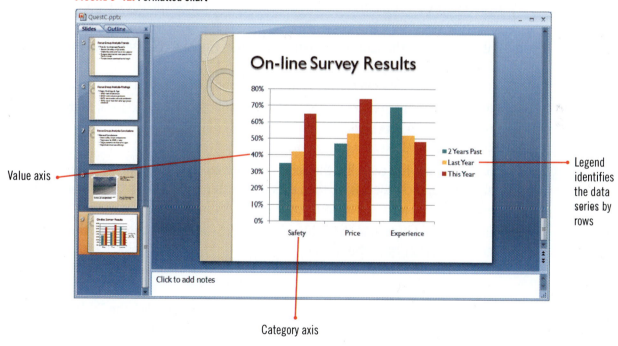

Value axis

Legend identifies the data series by rows

Category axis

Series in rows vs. series in columns

If you have difficulty visualizing what the Switch Row/Column command does, think about what is represented in the legend. **Series in Rows** means that the information in the datasheet rows will be on the Value or vertical axis and is the information shown in the legend. The column labels will be on the Category or horizontal axis. **Series in Columns** means that the information in the columns becomes the information shown on the Value axis and in the legend; the row labels will be on the horizontal or Category axis.

Inserting a Table

As you create your presentation, you may have some information that would look best organized in rows and columns. For example, if you wanted to compare the basic details of three different cruise tours side by side, a table is ideal for this type of information. Once you have created a table, two new tabs, the Table Tools Design tab and the Table Tools Layout tab, appear on the Ribbon. You can use the Design tab to apply color styles, change cell borders and add cell effects. Using the Layout tab, you can add rows and columns to your table, adjust the size of cells, and align text in the cells. You decide that a table best illustrates the new adventure tour series being proposed by Ellen.

STEPS

1. Verify that Slide 9 is selected, click the New Slide button list arrow in the Slides group, click Title Only, click the Insert tab on the Ribbon, then click the Table button in the Tables group

   The Insert Table gallery opens where you can drag the mouse to specify the number of columns and rows you need in the table.

2. Move the pointer over the grid to select a 4x3 cell area so that 4x3 Table appears in the gallery title bar, then click the lower right corner of the 4x3 grid

   A table with four columns and three rows appears on the slide, and the Table Tools Design tab opens on the Ribbon. The table has 12 cells. The insertion point is in the first cell of the table and is ready to accept text.

   > **QUICK TIP**
   > Pressing [Tab] when the insertion point is in the last cell of a table creates a new row.

3. Type Self Guided, press [Tab], type Family, press [Tab], type Cruise, press [Tab], type Extreme, then press [Tab]

   The text you typed appears in the top four cells of the table. Pressing [Tab] moves the insertion point to the next cell. Pressing [Enter] moves the insertion point to the next line in the cell. Pressing [Tab] in the last row, last column inserts a new row.

4. Enter the rest of the table information shown in Figure C-13, then drag the right-middle sizing handle slightly to the right

   The word Mediterranean now fits on one line. The table would look better if it were formatted differently.

5. Click the Table Styles More button ⏷ in the Table Styles group, scroll to the bottom of the gallery, then click Dark Style 1 – Accent 6

   The background and text color change to reflect the table style you applied.

   > **QUICK TIP**
   > You can change the height or width of any table cell by dragging its top or side borders.

6. Click the upper-left cell, click the Table Tools Layout tab, click the Select button in the Table group, click Select Row, then click the Center button ▤ in the Alignment group

   The text in the top row is centered horizontally in each cell.

7. Click the Select button in the Table group, click Select Table, then click the Center Vertically button ▤ in the Alignment group

   The text in the whole table is centered vertically within each cell. The table would look better if all the rows were the same height.

8. Click the Distribute Rows button ⊞ in the Cell Size group, click the Table Tools Design tab, then click the Effects button ▣▾ in the Table Styles group

   The Table Effects gallery opens. Apply a 3-D effect to the cells so that they stand out.

9. Point to Cell Bevel, click Cool Slant, drag the table to the center of the blank area of the slide, click the slide title placeholder, type Adventure Series, click a blank area of the slide, then save the presentation

   The effect makes the cells of the table stand out. Compare your screen with Figure C-14.

FIGURE C-13: The inserted table with data

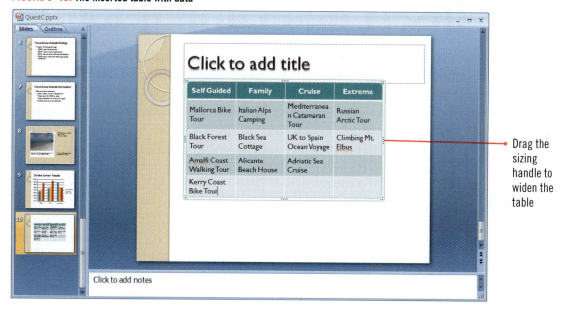

Drag the sizing handle to widen the table

FIGURE C-14: Formatted table

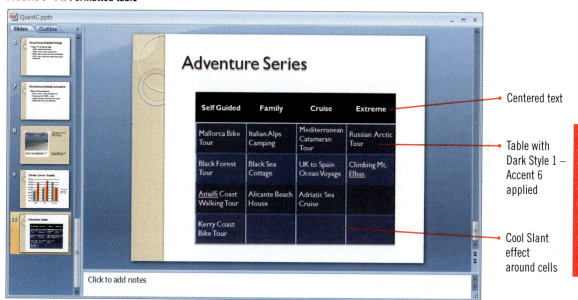

Centered text

Table with Dark Style 1 – Accent 6 applied

Cool Slant effect around cells

Saving slides as graphics

You can save PowerPoint slides as graphics and later use them in other presentations, in graphics programs, and on Web pages. Display the slide you want to save, click the Office button, then click Save As. In the Save As dialog box, click the Save as type list arrow, select the desired graphics format (for example, Web Page (*.htm;*.html), JPEG File Interchange Format (*.jpg), TIFF Tag Image Format (*.tif), or Device Independent Bitmap (*.bmp)), then name the file. Click Save, then click the desired option when the alert box appears asking if you want to save all the slides or only the current slide.

Insert and Format WordArt

As you work to create an interesting presentation, your goal should include making your slides visually appealing. Sometimes plain text can come across as dull and unexciting in a presentation. **WordArt** is a set of decorative text styles, or text effects, that you can apply to any text object to help direct the attention of your audience to a certain piece of information. You can use WordArt in two different ways: you can apply a WordArt text style to an existing text object that converts the text into WordArt, or you can create a new WordArt object. The WordArt text styles and effects include text shadows, reflections, glows, bevels, 3-D rotations, and transformations. Use WordArt to convert the QST tours tag line on Slide 1 so it is easier to see.

STEPS

1. **Click the Slide 1 thumbnail in the Slides tab, press [Shift], click the footer text object at the bottom of the slide, then drag the Zoom slider to the right until the Zoom percentage reaches 100%**

   Notice how the selected footer text object becomes the focal point as you zoom in. The footer text is hard to see and would look better with a WordArt style applied to it.

2. **Click the Drawing Tools Format tab, click the WordArt Styles More button ⬇, move your mouse over the WordArt styles in the gallery, then click Gradient Fill – Accent 6, Inner Shadow**

   The WordArt gallery displays all of the WordArt styles, and the Live Preview lets you see how each style would look if applied to the text.

3. **Click the Text Effects button 🅰 in the WordArt Styles group, point to Reflection, then click Tight Reflection, touching**

   The footer text object is now styled with a WordArt style and a reflection effect. You decide to increase the footer text font and give it a more prominent position on the slide.

4. **Click the Home tab on the Ribbon, click the Increase Font Size button 🅰 in the Font group twice, then drag the left-middle sizing handle to the left until the text is on one line**

   Now the footer text object is easier to read.

5. **Position ⬚ over the edge of the text object, drag to position the text object to match Figure C-15**

6. **Click a blank area of the slide, click the Fit slide to current window button ⬚ in the status bar**

   The slide returns to its original zoom percentage of 66%.

7. **Click the Slide Show button 🖥 on the status bar, view the presentation, press [Esc] at the end of the slide show, then click the Slide Sorter button 🔲 on the status bar**

   Figure C-16 shows the final presentation.

8. **Add your name as a footer to the notes and handouts, save your changes, print the presentation as handouts (four per page), then exit PowerPoint**

FIGURE C-15: Footer text converted to WordArt

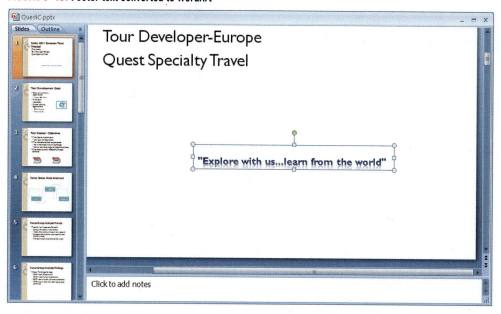

FIGURE C-16: Completed presentation in Slide Sorter view

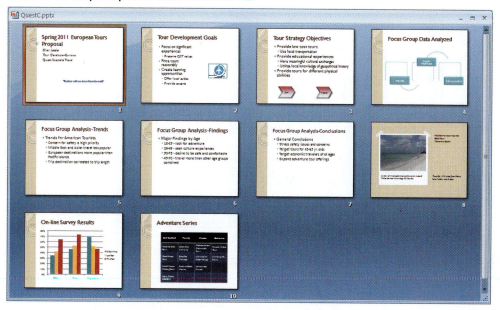

PowerPoint 2007

Using content templates from the Web

When you create a presentation, you have the option of using one of the many design themes supplied with PowerPoint, or you can use a template from the Microsoft Office Online Web site. These templates are designed and formatted with sample text, background and text colors, pictures, charts, and other graphic elements. To access a template from the Microsoft Office Online Web site, you need to be connected to the Internet, then click the Microsoft Office button. Click New to open the New Presentation dialog box. Click one of the template categories in the Microsoft Office Online template list in the left pane, then download and save the template in PowerPoint. Some of the template categories have subcategories that you need to select to display the individual templates. If you don't have access to the Internet or if you want to view more template choices, you can select one of the installed PowerPoint templates. In the New Presentation dialog box, click Installed Templates in the Template Categories list to select one of the installed templates.

Practice

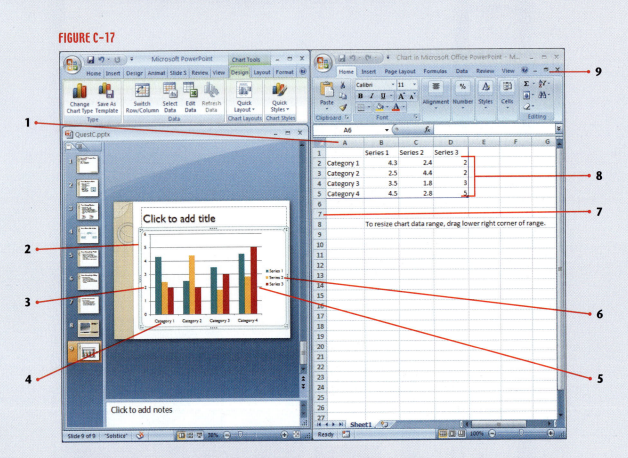

▼ CONCEPTS REVIEW

Label each element of the PowerPoint window shown in Figure C-17.

FIGURE C-17

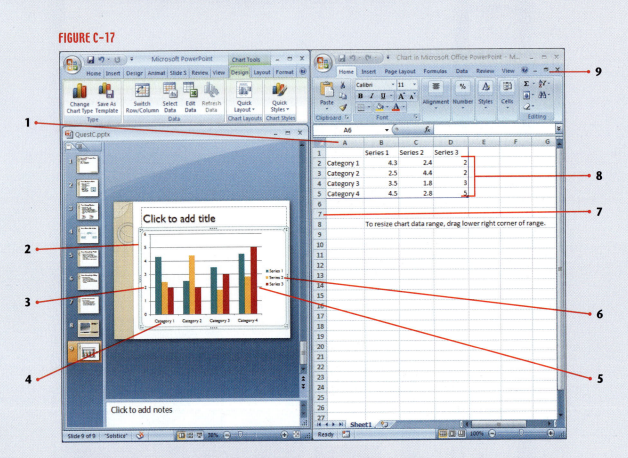

Match each term with the statement that best describes it.

10. Text label	a. The graphical representation of numerical data
11. Category axis	b. A set of decorative styles you can add to text
12. Value axis	c. Another name for the vertical axis in a chart
13. Chart	d. A specific type of text object used to enter a small phrase
14. WordArt	e. Another name for the horizontal axis in the chart

Select the best answer from the list of choices.

15. Which of the following statements about inserting text from Microsoft Word is *not* true?

a. Each line of inserted text is placed onto separate slides.

b. An outline structure is created in PowerPoint based on the Word styles used in the text.

c. PowerPoint can insert text that has tabs at the end of paragraphs.

d. You can create a new presentation based on inserted Word text.

16. What is the file index system that stores clip art, photographs, and movies called?

a. Microsoft Clip Organizer

b. Office Media Collections

c. Clip Art Index

d. WordArt Gallery

17. Hiding a portion of a picture or piece of clip art best describes which of the following actions?

a. Adjusting

b. Hiding

c. Styling

d. Cropping

18. Where is the numerical data located for a chart?

a. Table

b. Legend

c. Worksheet

d. Chart

19. An object that has its own data source and becomes a part of your presentation after you insert it best describes which of the following?

a. A Word outline

b. An embedded object

c. A WordArt object

d. A table

20. According to the book, which of the following objects is ideal to compare data side by side?

a. Table

b. Chart

c. Outline

d. Grid

21. A set of decorative text styles you apply to text describes which of the following items?

a. Text labels

b. Illustrations

c. WordArt

d. Gallery

22. What is a column of data in a worksheet called?

a. Column headings

b. Data series

c. Data series markers

d. Axis labels

▼ SKILLS REVIEW

1. Insert text from Microsoft Word.

a. Open the file **PPT C-4.pptx** from the drive and folder where you store your Data Files, then save it as **Blue Moon**. You will work to create the completed presentation as shown in Figure C-18.

b. Click Slide 3 in the Slides tab, then use the Slides from Outline command to insert the file **PPT C-5.docx** from the drive and folder where you store your Data Files.

c. In the Slides tab, drag Slide 5 above Slide 4.

d. In the Slides tab, delete Slide 7, Expansion Potential.

2. Insert clip art.

a. Select Slide 4, then change the slide layout to the Two Content slide layout.

FIGURE C-18

   b. Click the clip art icon in the right content placeholder, search for clip art using the keyword **leadership**, then insert the first clip in the Clip Art task pane.

   c. In the Size group on the Picture Tools Format Ribbon, use the Shape Width up arrow to change the width to 2.4".

   d. Click the Picture Border button, change the color of the clip art border to Gold, Accent 4.

   e. Click the Picture Border button, change the weight of the clip art border to 4½ pt.

   f. Click the Picture Effects button, point to 3-D Rotation, then click Off Axis 1 Right.

   g. Drag the clip art so the bottom lines up with the bottom of the text object, then save your changes.

3. Insert and style a picture.

   a. Select Slide 2, then insert the picture **PPT C-6.jpg**.

   b. Completely crop the light blue section off the top of the picture, then crop the right side of the picture about ¼".

   c. Drag the picture up so it is in the center of the blank area of the slide.

   d. Click the Recolor button, then change the picture color to Grayscale.

   e. Save your changes.

4. Insert a text box.

   a. On Slide 2, insert a text box below the picture.

   b. Type **Private submissions for music up 19%**.

   c. Delete the word for, then drag the word music after the word Private.

   d. Select the text object, then click the Shape Styles More button in the Shape Styles group on the Drawing Tools Format tab.

   e. Point to Other Theme Fills, then click Style 11.

   f. Center the text object under the picture.

5. Insert a chart.

   a. Go to Slide 3, 2009 CD Sales by Quarter, apply the Title and Content slide layout, then insert a Clustered Bar chart.

   b. Close Excel.

6. Enter and edit chart data.

   a. Show the chart data.

   b. Enter the data shown in Table C-2 into the worksheet.

   c. Delete the data in Column D, then close Excel.

   d. Change the chart style to Style 16 in the Chart Styles group.

   e. Save your changes.

TABLE C-2

	U.S. Sales	Int. Sales
1st Qtr	290,957	163,902
2nd Qtr	429,840	125,854
3rd Qtr	485,063	135,927
4th Qtr	365,113	103,750

7. Insert a table.

   a. Add a new slide after Slide 3 with the Title and Content layout.

   b. Add the slide title **New Subscription Plans**.

   c. Insert a table with 3 columns and 6 rows.

   d. Enter the information shown in Table C-3, then change the table style to Light Style 2 – Accent 1. (*Hint*: Use the Copy and Paste commands to enter duplicate information in the table.)

   e. Center the text in the top row.

TABLE C-3

Basic	Standard	Premium
$1.25 per download	$4.99 per month	$12.95 per month
Unlimited downloads	Max. 12 downloads	Max. 35 downloads
Limited access	Unlimited access	Unlimited access
Online registration	Online registration	Online registration
High-speed connection recommended	High-speed connection required	High-speed connection required

    f. In the Table Tools Layout tab, distribute the table rows.

    g. Save your changes.

8. Insert and format WordArt.

    a. Go to Slide 2, then select the bulleted list text object.

    b. Apply the WordArt style Fill – Accent 2, Warm Matte Bevel.

    c. View the presentation in Slide Show view, then save your changes.

    d. Add your name as a footer to the notes and handouts, print the slides as handouts (3 slides per page).

    e. Save your work, close the file, and exit PowerPoint.

▼ INDEPENDENT CHALLENGE 1

You are a financial management consultant for Casey Investments, located in St. Louis, Missouri. One of your responsibilities is to create standardized presentations on different financial investments for use on the company Web site. As part of the presentation for this meeting, you insert some clip art, add a text box, and insert a chart.

    a. Open the file PPT C-7.pptx from the drive and folder where you store your Data Files, then save it as **Casey**.

    b. Add your name as the footer on all notes and handouts, then apply the Oriel Design Theme.

    c. Insert a clustered column chart on Slide 6, then enter the data in Table C-4 into the worksheet.

    d. Format the chart using Style 27.

Advanced Challenge Exercise

    ■ Click the Chart Tools Layout tab, click the Legend button, then click Show Legend at Top.

    ■ Click the Chart Tools Format tab, then click the Current Selection list arrow in the Current Selection group, then click Series "3 Year."

    ■ Click the Shape Fill button list arrow, then click the Orange color under Standard Colors.

TABLE C-4

	1 year	3 year	5 year	7 year
Bonds	4.2%	5.2%	7.9%	6.5%
Stocks	6.9%	8.2%	7.2%	9.6%
Mutual Funds	4.6%	6.0%	7.4%	11.4%

    e. Insert clip art of a set of scales on Slide 2, then format as necessary. (*Hint*: Use the keyword scales to search for clips.)

    f. On Slide 3, use the Align, and Distribute commands on the Drawing Tools Format tab in the Arrange group to align and distribute the objects so that the shapes are aligned on top and distributed horizontally.

    g. Spell check the presentation, then save it.

    h. View the slide show. Make changes if necessary.

    i. The final presentation should look like Figure C-19.

    j. Print the slides as handouts (6 slides per page), then close the presentation, and exit PowerPoint.

FIGURE C-19

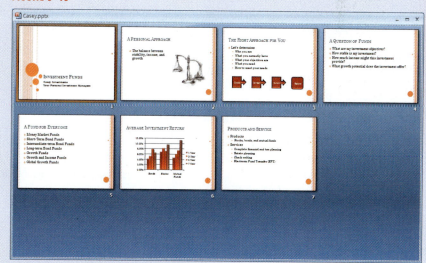

▼ INDEPENDENT CHALLENGE 2

You work for Alcom Home Systems, a company based out of Colorado Springs, Colorado that provides integrated data, security, and voice command systems for homes. You have been asked to enhance a marketing presentation on a new product that the company is going to promote at a large trade fair in Las Vegas. You work on completing a presentation for the show. You insert some clip art, add a text box, and insert a chart.

a. Start PowerPoint, open the file PPT C-8.pptx from the drive and folder where you store your Data Files, and save it as **Alcom**.

b. Add your name and today's date to Slide 1 in the Subtitle text box.

TABLE C-5

	Last Yr.	Current Yr.	Next Yr.
Traditional	91	85	74
Integrated	9	15	26

c. Organize the objects on Slide 2 using the Align, Distribute, and Group commands. Add and format additional shapes to enhance the presentation.

FIGURE C-20

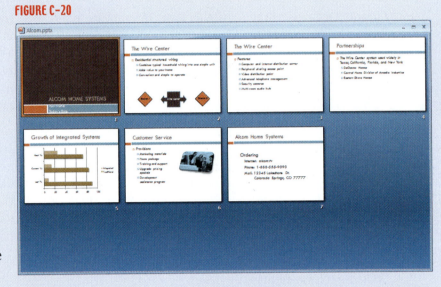

d. On Slide 3, style the picture, recolor the picture, and use a picture effect.

e. Apply the Median theme to the presentation.

f. Insert the Word document file **PPT C-9.docx** to create additional slides from an outline after Slide 2.

g. Create a new slide after Slide 4, title the slide **Growth of Integrated Systems**, then insert a chart.

h. Enter the data in Table C-5, then format the chart using at least two formatting commands. Be able to name which formatting commands you applied to the chart.

i. Insert a text box on the Alcom Home Systems slide (Slide 7). Create your own company contact and address information. Format the text box.

j. Spell check, then view the final slide show (refer to Figure C-20). Make any necessary changes.

k. Save the presentation, print the slides as handouts, close the file, and exit PowerPoint.

▼ INDEPENDENT CHALLENGE 3

You work for LearnSource Ltd., a company that produces instructional software to help people learn foreign languages. Once a year, LearnSource holds a meeting with their biggest client, the Department of State, to brief the government on new products and to receive feedback on existing products. Your boss has started a presentation and has asked you to look it over and add other elements to make it look better.

a. Start PowerPoint, open the file PPT C-10.pptx from the drive and folder where you store your Data Files, and save it as **LearnSource**.

b. Add an appropriate design theme to the presentation.

c. Insert the Word outline PPT C-11.docx after the Product Revisions slide.

d. Format the text so that the most important information is the most prominent.

e. Insert an appropriate table on a slide of your choice. Use your own information. (*Hint*: You can convert a bulleted list to a table.)

f. Add at least two appropriate shapes that emphasize slide content. Format the objects using shape styles. If appropriate, use the Align, Distribute, and Group commands to organize your shapes.

▼ INDEPENDENT CHALLENGE 3 (CONTINUED)

Advanced Challenge Exercise (*Internet connection required*)

- Open the Clip Art task pane, then click the Clip art on Office Online link to go to the Microsoft Office Online Web site.
- Insert an appropriate graphic.
- Format the graphic using Picture Tools Format tab.
- Be able to explain how you formatted the graphic object.

g. Spell check and view the final slide show (refer to Figure C-21). Make any necessary changes.

h. Add your name as footer text on the notes and handouts, save the presentation, then print the slides as handouts.

i. Save and close the file, and exit PowerPoint.

FIGURE C-21

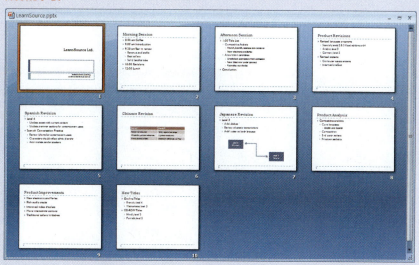

▼ REAL LIFE INDEPENDENT CHALLENGE

You are on the Foreign Exchange Commission at your college and one of your responsibilities is to present information on past foreign student exchanges to different organizations on and off campus. You need to create a pictorial presentation that highlights a trip to a different country. Create a presentation using your own pictures or photographs given to you with permission by a friend.

Note: Three photographs (PPT C-12.jpg, PPT C-13.jpg, and PPT C-14.jpg,) from Dijon, France are provided, if necessary to help you complete this Independent Challenge.

a. Start PowerPoint, create a new blank presentation, and save it as **Exchange** to the drive and folder where you store your Data Files.

b. Locate and insert the pictures you want to use. Place one picture on each slide using the Content with Caption slide layout.

c. Add information about each picture in the text placeholder and enter a slide title. If you use the pictures provided, research Dijon, France using the Internet for relevant information to place on the slides. (*Internet connection required*)

d. Apply an appropriate design theme.

e. Apply an appropriate title and your name to the title slide. Spell check, then view the final slide show (refer to Figure C-22).

f. Add a slide number to the slides and your name as footer text to the notes and handouts, save the presentation, then print the slides and notes pages (if any).

g. Save your work, close the file, and exit PowerPoint.

FIGURE C-22

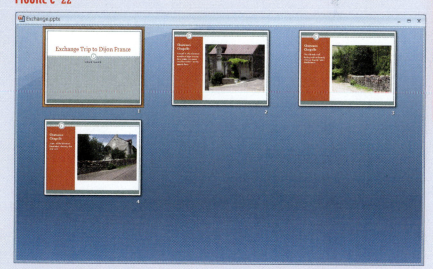

▼ VISUAL WORKSHOP

Create a one-slide presentation that looks like Figure C-23. The slide layout shown in Figure C-23 is a specific layout designed for pictures. Insert the picture file PPT C-6.jpg to complete this presentation. Add your name as footer to the slide, save the presentation as **Guitar Lessons** to the drive and folder where you store your Data Files, then print the slide.

FIGURE C-23

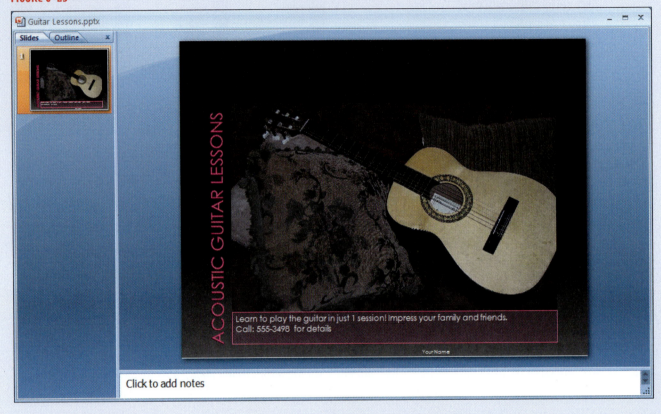

Finishing a Presentation

Files You Will Need:

PPT D-1.pptx
PPT D-2.jpg
PPT D-3.pptx
PPT D-4.jpg
PPT D-5.pptx
PPT D-6.pptx
PPT D-7.pptx
PPT D-8.pptx

Though not required, having a consistent professional-looking theme throughout your presentation is optimal if you want to peak and retain your audience's interest in the subject matter you are presenting. PowerPoint helps you achieve a consistent look by providing ways to customize your slides' layout and background. Once you are finished working with the text and other objects of your presentation, you are ready to apply slide show effects, which determine the way the slides and objects on the slides appear in Slide Show view. Ellen has reviewed the presentation and is pleased with the slides you created for the Quest Specialty Travel presentation. You are ready to finalize the layouts and add effects to make the presentation interesting to watch.

OBJECTIVES

Understand masters

Customize background style

Use slide show commands

Set slide show transitions and timings

Set slide animation effects

Inspect a presentation

Evaluate a presentation

Create a design template

Understanding Masters

Each presentation in PowerPoint has a set of **masters**, which store information, including the position and size of text and content placeholders, text styles, background colors, effects, animations, and theme colors. There are three Master views: Slide Master view, Handout Master view, and Notes Master view. Changes made to the Slide Master are reflected on all the slides, changes made to the Notes Master are reflected in the Notes Page view, and changes made to the Handout Master are reflected when you print your presentation using one of the Handout print options. Design elements that you place on the Slide Master appear on every slide in the presentation. For example, you could insert a company logo in the upper-right corner of the slide master and that logo would then appear on every slide in your presentation. Each Slide Master has associated layouts. Changes made to a layout affect all slides that have that layout. You want to add the company logo to the presentation, so you open your presentation and examine the slide master.

STEPS

1. **Start PowerPoint, open the presentation PPT D-1.pptx from the drive and folder where you store your Data Files, save the presentation as QuestD, click the View tab on the Ribbon, then click the Arrange All button in the Window group**

   The title slide of the presentation appears.

QUICK TIP

You can press and hold [Shift] and click the Normal button on the status bar to display the slide master.

2. **Click the Slide Master button in the Presentation Views group, then click the Solstice Slide Master thumbnail (first thumbnail) in the left pane**

   The Slide Master view appears with the slide master displayed in the Slide pane as shown in Figure D-1. This master slide is the theme master slide (the Solstice theme in this case). Each master text placeholder identifies the font size, style, color, and position of text placeholders on the slide in Normal view. For example, the Master title placeholder, labeled "Click to edit Master title style," is positioned at the top of the slide and uses a brown, shadowed, 44 pt, Gill Sans MT font. Any objects you place on the slide master will appear on all slides in the presentation. The slide layouts located below the master slide thumbnail in the left pane follow the information in the master slide and changes you make to this master slide, including font changes, are reflected in all of the slide layouts. Each slide layout in the presentation can be modified independently. Each theme comes with its own associated slide masters.

QUICK TIP

When working with slide layouts, you can right-click the thumbnail to open a shortcut list of commands.

3. **Point to each slide layout in the left pane, then click the Title Only Layout thumbnail**

   As you point to each slide layout, a ScreenTip appears which identifies each slide layout by name and lists if any of the slides in the presentation are currently using the layout. Three slides are using the Title Only Layout, Slide 4, Slide 9, and Slide 10.

4. **Click the Solstice Slide Master thumbnail, click the Insert tab on the Ribbon, then click the Picture button in the Illustrations group**

   The Insert Picture dialog box opens.

5. **Select the picture file PPT D-2.jpg from the drive and folder where you store your Data Files, then click Insert**

   The QST graphic logo appears on the slide master and will appear on all slides in the presentation. The graphic is too large and needs to be repositioned on the slide so you reduce its size and move it to a better location on the slide.

6. **Click the Shape Width down arrow in the Size group until 1.1" appears, then drag the graphic to the upper left corner of the slide**

   Compare your screen to Figure D-2.

7. **Click the Normal button 🔲 on the status bar, then save your changes**

FIGURE D-1: Slide Master view

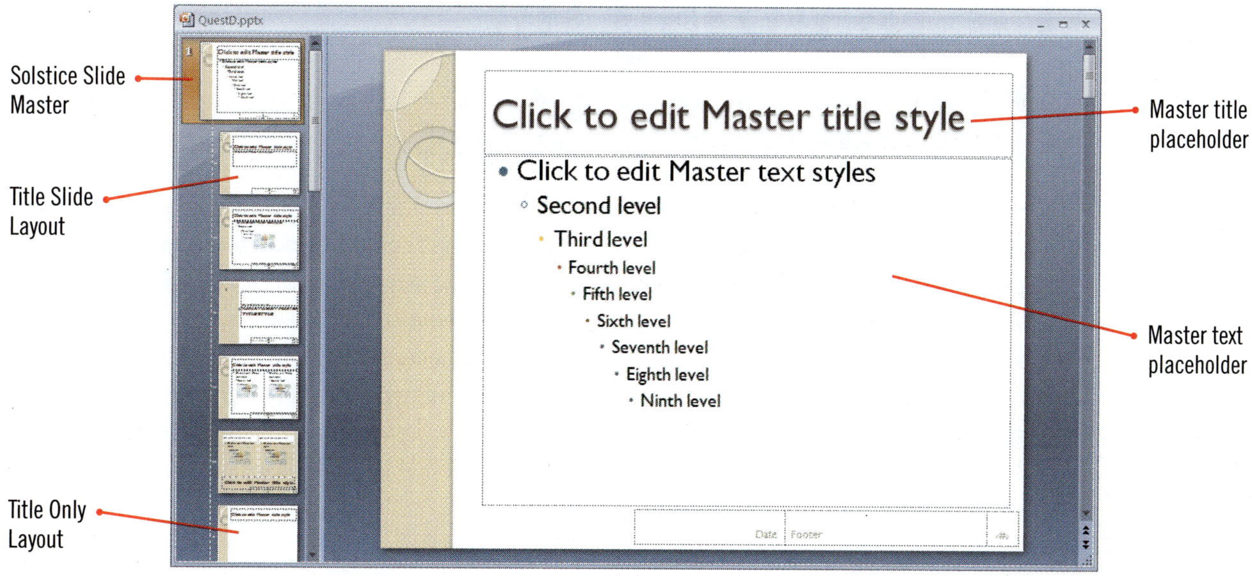

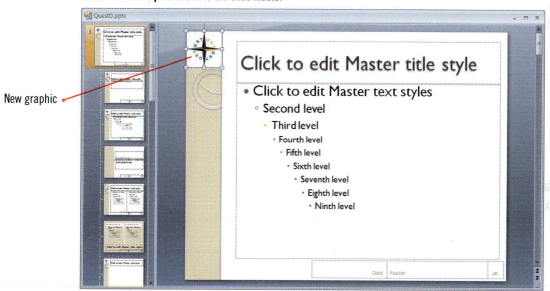

Solstice Slide Master

Title Slide Layout

Title Only Layout

Master title placeholder

Master text placeholder

FIGURE D-2: Graphic added to the slide master

New graphic

Create custom slide layouts

As you work with PowerPoint, you may find that you need to develop a customized slide layout. For example, you may need to create presentations for a client that has slides that display four pictures with a caption underneath each picture. To make everyone's job easier, you create a custom slide layout that includes only the placeholders needed for that particular slide layout. To create a custom slide layout, open Slide Master view, click the Insert Layout button in the Edit Master group. A new slide layout appears in the Slide pane. You can choose to add several different placeholders including

Content, Text, Picture, Chart, Table, SmartArt, Media, and Clip Art. Click the Insert Placeholder button arrow in the Master Layout group, click the placeholder you want to add, drag + to create the placeholder, then position the placeholder on the slide. In Slide Master view, you can add or delete placeholders in any of the slide layouts. You can rename a custom slide layout by clicking the Rename button in the Edit Master group and entering a descriptive name to better identify the layout.

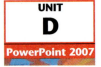
Customizing the Background Style

Every slide in a PowerPoint presentation has a **background**, the area behind the text and graphics. You modify the background to enhance the slides using images and color. A **background graphic** is an object placed on the slide master. You can quickly change the background appearance by applying a background style, which is a set of color variations derived from the theme colors. **Theme colors** are a set of twelve coordinated colors that determine the colors for all slide elements in your presentation including: slide background, text and lines, shadows, title text, fills, accents, and hyperlinks. Every theme, such as Civic and Solstice, has its own set of theme colors. See Table D-1 for a description of the theme colors. The QST presentation needs some design enhancements. You decide to modify the background of the slides in the presentation by applying a background style.

STEPS

1. **Click the Design tab on the Ribbon, then click the Background Styles button in the Background group**

   A gallery of background styles opens. Review the different backgrounds using Live Preview.

QUICK TIP

To apply a new background style to only selected slides, select the slides on the Slides tab or in Slide Sorter view, right-click the background style in the Background Styles gallery, then click Apply to Selected Slides.

---

2. **Move the pointer over each style in the gallery, then click Style 6**

   Figure D-3 shows the new background on Slide 1 of the presentation. Even though you are working in Normal view, the new background style is applied to every slide in the presentation and to the master slide and master slide layouts. The new background style did not appear over the whole slide, which indicates there is a background graphic on the slide master that is preventing you from seeing the entire slide background.

3. **Click the Hide Background Graphics check box in the Background group**

   For the selected slide, all the background graphics are hidden from view and only the text objects on the slide remain visible.

4. **Click the Hide Background Graphics check box to display the background graphics, click the Background Styles button, then click Format Background**

   The Format Background dialog box opens.

QUICK TIP

You can also apply a gradient background style to a shape by right-clicking the shape, then clicking Format Shape in the shortcut menu.

---

5. **Click the Type list arrow, click Linear, click the Direction button, click Linear Down, click Apply to All, then click Close**

   The gradient fill of the background style now progresses from dark to light starting at the bottom of the slide and moving to the top. You need to fix the background color of the QST logo graphic so it does not obstruct the slide background graphics.

6. **Press [Shift], click the Normal button on the status bar, click the Solstice Slide Master thumbnail in the left pane, then click the QST graphic**

   The graphic is selected in the Slide Master view.

7. **Click the Picture Tools Format tab on the Ribbon, click the Recolor button in the Adjust group, click Set Transparent Color, then move the pointer over the slide**

   The pointer changes to the transparent pointer.

TROUBLE

If the white background does not become transparent, click the Undo button, then repeat the step.

---

8. **Position over the white background of the QST logo graphic, then click**

   The white background of the QST graphic becomes transparent and the slide background appears behind the graphic.

9. **Click the Normal button on the status bar, then save your work**

   Compare your screen to Figure D-4.

FIGURE D-3: Slide with new background style applied

New background style is applied to all the slides

New background style

New background style did not appear here

FIGURE D-4: Finished slide

Graphic with transparent background

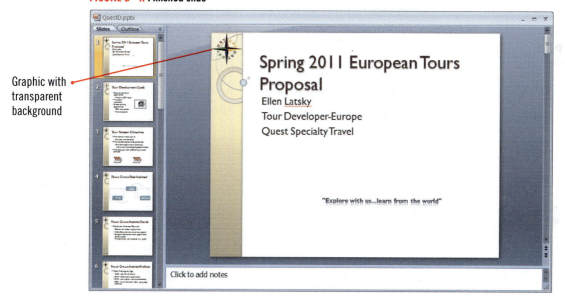

TABLE D-1: Theme colors

scheme element	description
Background color	Color of the slide's background; fills the slide
Text and lines color	Used for any typed characters and drawn lines; contrasts with the background color
Shadows color	The shadow color for text and other objects; generally a darker shade of the background color
Title text color	Used for slide title; like the text and line colors and contrasts with the background color
Fills color	Used to fill shapes and other objects with color. Contrasts with both the background and the text and line colors
Accent colors	Colors used for other objects on slides, such as bullets
Accent and hyperlink colors	Colors used for accent objects and for hyperlinks you insert
Accent and followed hyperlink color	Color used for accent objects and for hyperlinks after they have been clicked

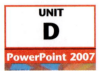

Using Slide Show Commands

With PowerPoint, you can show a presentation on any compatible computer using Slide Show view. As you've seen, Slide Show view fills your computer screen with the slides of the presentation, showing them one at a time. Once the presentation is in Slide Show view, you can use a number of slide show options to tailor the show to meet your needs. For example, you can draw, or **annotate**, on slides or jump to different slides in other parts of the presentation. ▰▰▰ Ellen wants you to learn how to run a slide show and use the slide show options so you can help her when she gives the presentation. You run the slide show of the presentation and practice using some of the custom slide show options.

STEPS

1. **Click the View tab on the Ribbon, then click the Slide Show button in the Presentation Views group**

   The first slide of the presentation fills the screen.

2. **Press [Spacebar]**

   Slide 2 appears on the screen. Pressing [Spacebar] or clicking the left mouse button is the easiest way to move through a slide show. See Table D-2 for other Slide Show view key commands. You can also use the Slide Show shortcut menu for on-screen navigation during a slide show.

3. **Right-click anywhere on the screen, point to Go to Slide on the shortcut menu, then click 8 Mediterranean Islands Bike Tour**

   The slide show jumps to Slide 8. You can highlight or emphasize major points in your presentation by annotating the slide during a slide show using one of PowerPoint's annotation tools.

4. **Move the pointer to the bottom left corner of the screen to display the Slide Show toolbar, click the Pen Options menu button 🖊, then click Highlighter**

   The pointer changes to the highlighter pointer ▮.

5. **Drag ▮ to highlight the text below the picture**

   Compare your screen to Figure D-5. While the annotation tool is visible, mouse clicks do not advance the slide show; however, you can still move to the next slide by pressing [Spacebar] or [Enter].

6. **Click the Pen Options menu button 🖊 on the Slide Show toolbar, click Erase All Ink on Slide, then press [Ctrl][A]**

   The annotations on Slide 8 are erased and the pointer returns to ▷ when you press [Ctrl][A].

7. **Click the Slide Show menu button ▤ on the Slide Show toolbar, point to Go to Slide, then click 10 Adventure Series on the menu**

   Slide 10 appears.

8. **Press [Home], then press [Enter] to advance through the slide show, then when you see the black slide at the end of the slide show, press [Spacebar]**

   You are returned to Normal view. The black slide indicates the end of the slide show.

FIGURE D-5: Slide 8 in Slide Show view with highlight annotations

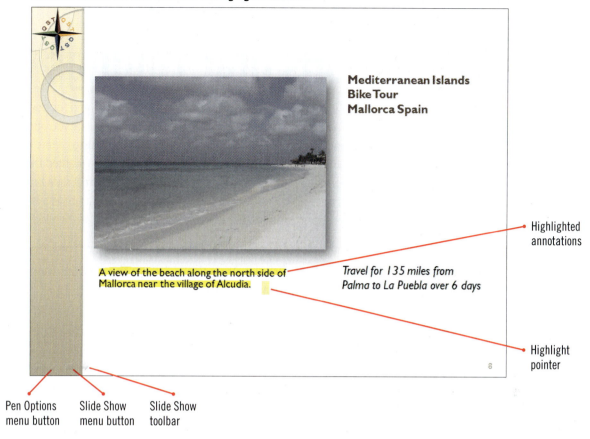

Mediterranean Islands
Bike Tour
Mallorca Spain

A view of the beach along the north side of Mallorca near the village of Alcudia.

Travel for 135 miles from Palma to La Puebla over 6 days

Highlighted annotations

Highlight pointer

Pen Options menu button

Slide Show menu button

Slide Show toolbar

TABLE D-2: Basic Slide Show keyboard controls

control	description
[Enter], [Spacebar], [PgDn], [N], [down arrow key], or [right arrow key]	Advances to the next slide
[E]	Erases the annotation drawing
[Home], [End]	Moves to the first or last slide in the slide show
[H]	Displays a hidden slide
[up arrow key] or [PgUp]	Returns to the previous slide
[W]	Changes the screen to white; press again to return
[S]	Pauses the slide show; press again to continue
[B]	Changes the screen to black; press again to return
[Ctrl][M]	Shows or hides annotations on the slide
[Ctrl][A]	Changes pointer to ⟲
[Esc]	Stops the slide show

Setting Slide Show Transitions and Timings

In a slide show, you can specify how each slide advances in and out of view, and for how long each slide appears on the screen. **Slide transitions** are the special visual and audio effects you apply to a slide that determine how it moves in and out of view during the slide show. **Slide timing**, refers to the amount of time a slide is visible on the screen. Typically, you would set slide timings if you wanted the presentation to automatically progress through the slides during a slide show. Setting the correct slide timing, in this case, is important because it determines how long each slide is visible. Each slide can have a different slide timing. You decide to set slide transitions and 8 second slide timings for all the slides.

STEPS

1. **Make sure Slide 1 is selected, click the Animations tab on the Ribbon, then point to each of the transition options in the Transition to This Slide group**

   A Live Preview of each transition is displayed on the slide. Transitions are organized by type into five groups.

2. **Click the More button in the Transition to This Slide group, then click Box In in the Wipes section (3rd row)**

   The new slide transition plays on the slide and a transition icon appears next to the slide thumbnail in the Slides tab as shown in Figure D-6. The slide transition would have more impact if it were slowed down.

3. **Click the Transition Speed list arrow in the Transition to This Slide group, then click Medium**

   The Box In slide transition plays again at the slower speed. You can apply this transition to all of the slides in the presentation.

4. **Click the Apply To All button in the Transition to This Slide group, then click the Slide Sorter button ⊞ on the status bar**

   All of the slides now have the Box In transition at the medium speed applied to them as identified by the transition icons located below each slide. The options under Advance Slide in the Transition to This Slide group determine how slides progress during a slide show—either by mouse click or automatically by slide timing.

5. **Click the Automatically After up arrow until 00.08 appears in the text box, then click the Apply To All button in the Transition to This Slide group**

   The timing between slides is 8 seconds as indicated by the time under each slide in Slide Sorter view. See Figure D-7. When you run the slide show, each slide will remain on the screen for 8 seconds. You can override a slide's timing and speed up the slide show by pressing [Spacebar], [Enter], or clicking the left mouse button during a slide show.

6. **Click Slide 8, click the Transition Sound list arrow in the Transition to This Slide group, then click Breeze**

   The Breeze sound will now play when Slide 8 appears during the slide show.

7. **Press [Home], click the Slide Show button ⬚ on the status bar, then watch the slide show advance automatically**

8. **When you see the black slide at the end of the slide show, press [Spacebar], then save your changes**

   The slide show ends and returns to Slide Sorter view with Slide 1 selected.

FIGURE D-6: Applied slide transition

Box In slide transition

More button

Transition icon

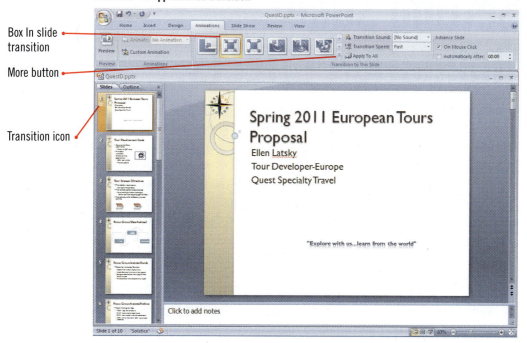

FIGURE D-7: Slide Sorter view showing applied transition and timing

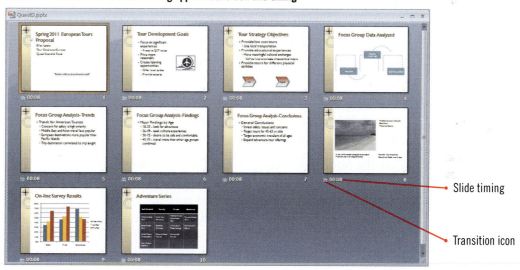

Slide timing

Transition icon

Rehearsing slide show timings

You can set different slide timings for each slide. For example, you can have the title slide appear for 20 seconds, the second slide for 1 minute, and so on. You can set timings by clicking the Rehearse Timings button in the Set Up group on the Slide Show tab. Slide Show view opens and the Rehearsal toolbar shown in Figure D-8 opens. It contains buttons to pause between slides and to advance to the next slide. After opening the Rehearsal toolbar, practice giving your presentation. PowerPoint keeps track of how long each slide appears and sets the timing accordingly. You can view your rehearsed timings in Slide Sorter view. The next time you run the slide show, you can use the timings you rehearsed.

FIGURE D-8: Rehearsal toolbar

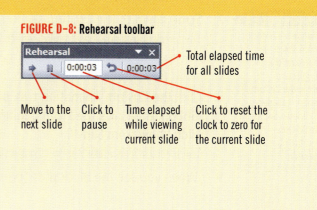

Total elapsed time for all slides

Move to the next slide

Click to pause

Time elapsed while viewing current slide

Click to reset the clock to zero for the current slide

Setting Slide Animation Effects

Animation effects let you control how the objects and main points in your presentation appear on the screen during a slide show. You can set custom animation effects or use one of several standard animation effects. For example, you can apply a Fade by 1st Level Paragraphs animation effect to bulleted text so that each first level bullet appears separately from the others. Using animation effects allows you to control how information flows and what information is emphasized. You can animate text, graphics, sounds, hyperlinks, SmartArt diagrams, charts and individual chart elements. The standard animation effects include Fade, Wipe, and Fly In and can be applied to any selected object. Custom animation effects are organized into four categories, which provide you a wide range of animation choices, such as Ease In and Flicker. Ellen wants you to animate the text and graphics of several slides in the presentation using animation effects.

STEPS

1. Verify that the **Animations tab** is selected on the Ribbon, double-click **Slide 2** to view it in Normal view, then click the **body text** object

   The bullets in the text object can be animated to appear one at a time during a slide show.

2. Click the **Animate list arrow** in the Animations group, then click **By 1st Level Paragraphs** in the Fade section

   As you click the animation option a Live Preview of the Box In transition and the Fade animation effect plays.

3. Click the **Slide Show button** 🖥 on the status bar, then press **[Esc]** when you see Slide 3

   The Fade animation effect, which begins after the slide transition effect, is active on Slide 2. You can also animate other objects on a slide by setting custom animations.

4. Make sure **Slide 3** is selected, click the grouped **arrow object** on the slide, then click the **Custom Animation button** in the Animations group

   The Custom Animation task pane opens.

5. Click the **Add Effect button** in the Custom Animation task pane, then point to **Entrance**

   A submenu of Entrance animation effects appears next to a menu of four animation categories, Entrance, Emphasis, Exit, and Motion Paths as shown in Figure D-9. An Entrance animation effect causes an object to enter the slide with an effect; an Emphasis animation effect causes an object already visible on the slide to have an effect; an Exit animation effect causes an object to leave the slide with an effect; and a Motion Paths animation effect causes an object to move on a specified path on the slide.

6. Click **More Effects**

   The Add Entrance Effect dialog box opens. All of the effects in this dialog box allow an object to enter the slide using a special effect.

7. Scroll down to the **Exciting section**, click **Glide**, then click **OK**

   The arrow object now has the glide effect applied to it as shown in Figure D-10. Notice that the arrow object now has an animation tag and is listed in the Custom Animation task pane as the first object to be animated on the slide. **Animation tags** identify the order in which objects are animated during slide show.

8. Click the Custom Animation task pane **Close button** ✕, click the **Slide Show tab** on the Ribbon, then click the **From Beginning button** in the Start Slide Show group to run the Slide Show from Slide 1

   The special effects make the presentation more interesting to view.

9. When you see the black slide, press **[Spacebar]**, then save your changes

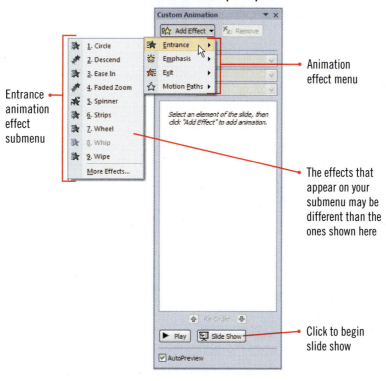

Animation effect menu

Entrance animation effect submenu

The effects that appear on your submenu may be different than the ones shown here

Click to begin slide show

FIGURE D-10: Screen showing animated arrow object

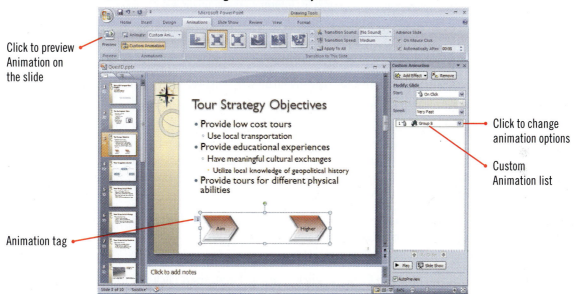

Click to preview Animation on the slide

Click to change animation options

Custom Animation list

Animation tag

Presentation checklist

You should always rehearse your slide show. If possible, rehearse your presentation in the room and with the computer that you will use. Use the following checklist to prepare for the slide show:

- Is **PowerPoint** or **PowerPoint Viewer** installed on the computer?
- Is your **presentation file** on the hard drive of the computer you will be using? Try putting a shortcut for the file on the desktop. Do you have a backup copy of your presentation file on a removable storage device?
- Is the **projection device** working correctly? Can the slides be seen from the back of the room?

- Do you know how to control **room lighting** so that the audience can see both your slides and their handouts and notes? You may want to designate someone to control the lights if the controls are not close to you.
- Will the **computer** be situated so you can advance and annotate the slides yourself? If not, designate someone to advance them for you.
- Do you have enough copies of your **handouts**? Bring extras. Decide when to hand them out, or whether you prefer to have them waiting at the audience members' seats when they enter.

Inspecting a Presentation

Reviewing your presentation can be an important step, not only to find and fix errors, but also to locate and delete private company or personal information and document properties you do not want to share with others. If you share presentations with others, especially over the Internet, it is a good idea to inspect the presentation file using the Document Inspector. The **Document Inspector** looks for hidden data and personal information that is stored in the file itself or in the document properties. Document properties, also known as **metadata**, includes specific data about the presentation, such as the author's name, sub-ject matter, title, who saved the file last, and when the file was created. Other types of information the Document Inspector can locate and remove include: presentation notes, comments, ink annotations, invis-ible on-slide content, off-slide content, and custom XML data. QST has strict rules about revealing personal and company information in documents. You decide to view and add some document properties, inspect your presentation file, and learn about the Mark as Final command.

STEPS

1. **Click the Office button , point to Prepare, then click Properties**

   The Document Properties pane opens showing the file location and the title of the presentation. Now enter some descriptive data for this presentation file.

2. **Enter the data shown in Figure D-11, then click the Properties pane Close button**

   This data provides detailed information about the presentation file that you can use to identify and organ-ize your file. You can also use this information as search criteria to locate the file at a later time. You now use the Document Inspector to search for information you might want to delete in the presentation.

3. **Click , point to Prepare, click Inspect Document, click Yes to save the changes to the document, then read the dialog box**

   The Document Inspector dialog box opens. The Document Inspector searches the presentation file for six different types of information that you might want removed from the presentation before sending it.

4. **Make sure all of the check boxes are selected, then click Inspect**

   The presentation file is reviewed and the Document Inspector dialog box displays the results shown in Figure D-12. Notice that there are three items found: document properties in the Document Properties pane, an off slide object that you created and didn't use, and some reminder notes you wrote yourself in the Notes pane on Slides 8, 9, and 10. You decide to leave the document properties alone but delete the off-slide object, and the notes in the Notes pane for all of the slides.

5. **Click the Off-Slide Content Remove All button, click the Presentation Notes Remove All button, then click Close**

   All of those items are removed from the presentation.

6. **Click , point to Prepare, click Mark as Final, then click OK in the alert dialog box**

   A dialog box opens. Be sure to read the dialog box to understand what happens to the file and how to recog-nize a marked-as-final presentation. You decide to proceed with this operation.

7. **Click OK, click the Home tab on the Ribbon, click the Slide 1 thumbnail in the Slides pane, then click anywhere in the title text object**

   Notice that the commands on the Ribbon are dimmed as shown in Figure D-13. Because you marked the file as final, the file is read-only. A **read-only** file is one that can't be edited or modified in any way. Anyone who has received a read-only presentation can edit the presentation by removing the mark as final status. You still want to work on the presentation, so you remove the mark as final status.

8. **Click , point to Prepare, click Mark as Final, then save your changes**

   The commands on the Ribbon are active again, and the file can now be modified.

FIGURE D-11: Document Properties pane

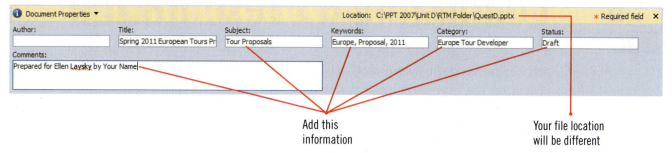

Add this
information

Your file location
will be different

FIGURE D-12: Document Inspector dialog box

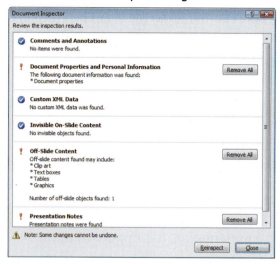

FIGURE D-13: Marked-as-final presentation

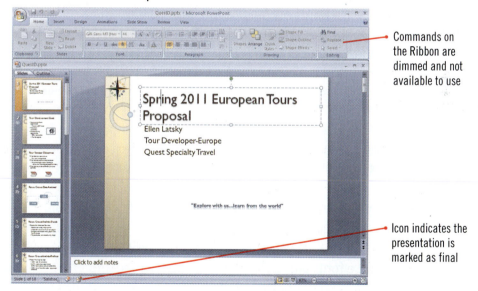

Commands on
the Ribbon are
dimmed and not
available to use

Icon indicates the
presentation is
marked as final

Digitally sign a presentation

So what is a digital signature and why would you want to use one in PowerPoint? A digital signature is similar to a hand-written signature in that it authenticates your document; however, a digital signature, unlike a hand-written signature, is created using computer cryptography and is not visible within the presentation itself. There are three primary reasons you would add a digital signature to a presentation: one, to authenticate the signer of the document; two, to assure that the content of the presentation has not been changed since it was signed; and three, to assure the origin of the signed document. To add a digital signature, click the Office button, point to Prepare, click Add a Digital Signature, then follow the dialog boxes.

Evaluating a Presentation

As you create a presentation, keep in mind that a good design requires preparation. An effective presentation is focused and visually appealing—easy for the speaker to present and simple for the audience to understand. The visual elements (colors, graphics, and text) can strongly influence the audience's attention and interest and can determine the success of your presentation. See Table D-3 for general information on the impact a visual presentation has on an audience. You know Ellen will critique your presentation, so you take the time to evaluate your presentation's effectiveness.

STEPS

1. **Click the Slide Show button ☐ on the status bar, then press [Spacebar] when the slide show finishes**

2. **Click the Slide Sorter button ☐ on the status bar**
    You decide that Slide 8 should come after Slide 10.

3. **Drag Slide 8 to the right side of Slide 10, then save your changes**
    Slide 8 is moved to the end of the presentation. The final presentation is shown in Slide Sorter view. Compare your screen to Figure D-14.

4. **Double-click Slide 1, then evaluate your presentation according to the guidelines below**
    Figure D-15 shows a poorly designed slide. Contrast this slide with your presentation as you review the following guidelines.

When evaluating a presentation, it is important to:

*   **Keep your message focused**
    Don't put every point you plan to say on your presentation slides. Keep the audience anticipating further explanations to the key points shown in the presentation.

*   **Keep your text concise**
    Limit each slide to six words per line and six lines per slide. Use lists and symbols to help prioritize your points visually. Your presentation text provides only the highlights; use notes to give more detailed information. Your presentation focuses attention on the key issues and you supplement the information with further explanation and details during your presentation.

*   **Keep the design simple, easy to read, and appropriate for the content**
    A design theme makes the presentation consistent. If you design your own layout, keep it simple and use design elements sparingly. Use similar design elements consistently throughout the presentation; otherwise, your audience may get confused.

*   **Choose attractive colors that make the slide easy to read**
    Use contrasting colors for slide background and text to make the text readable. If you are giving an on-screen presentation, you can use almost any combination of colors that look good together.

*   **Choose fonts and styles that are easy to read and emphasize important text**
    As a general rule, use no more than two fonts in a presentation and vary the font size, using nothing smaller than 24 points. Use bold and italic attributes selectively.

*   **Use visuals to help communicate the message of your presentation**
    Commonly used visuals include clip art, photographs, charts, worksheets, tables, and movies. Whenever possible, replace text with a visual, but be careful not to overcrowd your slides. White space on your slides is OK!

FIGURE D-14: The final presentation in Slide Sorter view

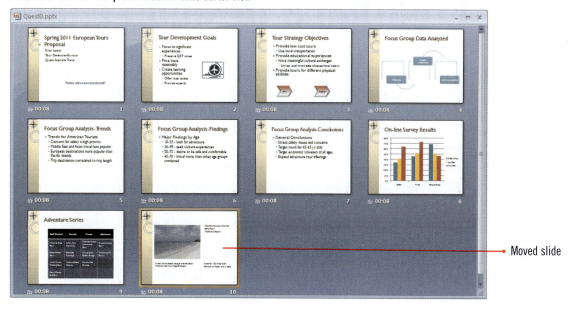
Moved slide

FIGURE D-15: A poorly designed slide

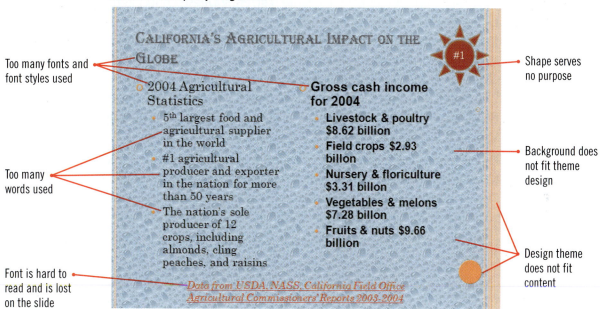

Too many fonts and font styles used

Too many words used

Font is hard to read and is lost on the slide

Shape serves no purpose

Background does not fit theme design

Design theme does not fit content

TABLE D-3: Audience impact from a visual presentation

impact	description
Visual reception	75% of all environmental stimuli is received through visual reception
Learning	55% of what an audience learns comes directly from visual messages
Retention	Combining visual messages with verbal messages can increase memory retention by as much as 30%
Presentation goals	You are twice as likely to achieve your communication objectives using a visual presentation
Meeting length	You are likely to decrease the average meeting length by 26% when you use a visual presentation

Source: Presenters Online, www.presentersonline.com

Creating a Design Template

When planning the design of your presentation, keep in mind that you are not limited to using just the standard themes PowerPoint provides or the ones you find on the Web. You can customize your presentation using a template. A **template** is a type of presentation file that contains custom design information made to the slide master, slide layouts, and theme. You can create a new template from a blank presentation, or you can modify an existing PowerPoint presentation that you have access to and save it as a template. If you modify an existing presentation, you can keep, change, or delete any color, graphic, or font as necessary. When you are finished creating a new presentation or modifying an existing presentation, you can save it as a template file, which adds the .potx extension to the filename. You can then use your template presentation as the basis for new presentations. You are finished working on your presentation for now. You want to save the presentation as a template so you and others can use it.

STEPS

QUICK TIP
Presentations saved to the Templates folder appear in the New Presentation dialog box under My Templates.

1. **Click the Office button , point to Save As, click Other Formats, click the Save as type list arrow, then click PowerPoint Template (*.potx)**

   Because this is a template, PowerPoint automatically opens the Templates folder on your hard drive as shown in Figure D-16.

2. **Use the Favorite Link or Folders pane to locate the drive and folder where you store your Data Files, click to select the filename (currently QuestD.potx) in the File name list box, type QuestD Template, then click Save**

   The presentation is saved as a PowerPoint template to the drive and folder where you store your Data Files, and the new template presentation appears in the PowerPoint window. The filename in the title bar has a .potx extension which identifies this presentation as a template.

3. **Click the Slide Sorter button on the status bar, click Slide 3, press and hold [Shift], click Slide 10, release [Shift], then click the Cut button in the Clipboard group**

   Slides 3 through 10 are deleted.

4. **Double-click Slide 2, press and hold [Shift], click the body text object, click the title text object, right-click the clip art object, release [Shift], then click Cut**

   The clip art object and the text in the text objects are deleted. Sometimes templates have sample text.

5. **Type Slide Title Here, click the content placeholder, type Bulleted list, press [Enter], press [Tab], type Bulleted list, click the Layout button in the Slides group, then click Title and Content**

   Sample text replaces the text, and the slide layout changes to the Title and Content slide layout.

6. **Click the Slide 1 thumbnail in the Slides tab, press [Shift], select the three text objects on the slide, then press [Delete]**

   The WordArt object and the text in the text objects are deleted.

7. **Click the title text placeholder, type QST Template, click the subtitle placeholder, type Subtitle text here, then save your changes**

8. **Click the View tab, then click the Slide Sorter button in the Presentation Views group**

   Figure D-17 shows the final template presentation in Slide Sorter view.

9. **Save your work, print the template presentation as handouts (2 per page), close the presentation, then exit PowerPoint**

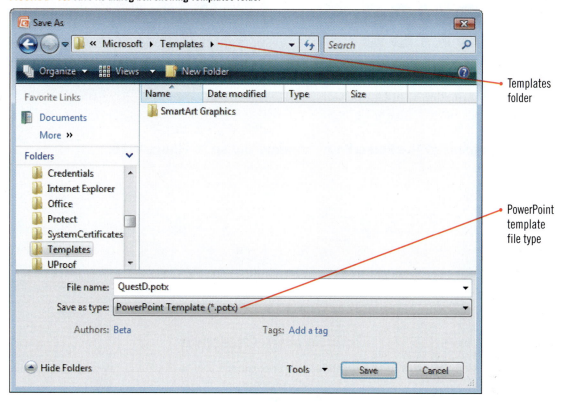

Templates folder

PowerPoint template file type

Applying a theme from another presentation

When you apply a theme from one presentation to another, you automatically apply the master layouts, colors and fonts over the existing presentation's theme. To apply a theme from another presentation, open the presentation you want to apply the theme to, click the Design tab, then click the Themes group More button.

Click Browse for Themes, use the Favorite Links or Folders pane to navigate to the presentation whose theme you want to apply. The presentation you select can be a regular presentation or a template with the .potx extension. Click the presentation name, then click Apply.

Practice

▼ CONCEPTS REVIEW

Label each element of the PowerPoint window shown in Figure D-18.

FIGURE D-18

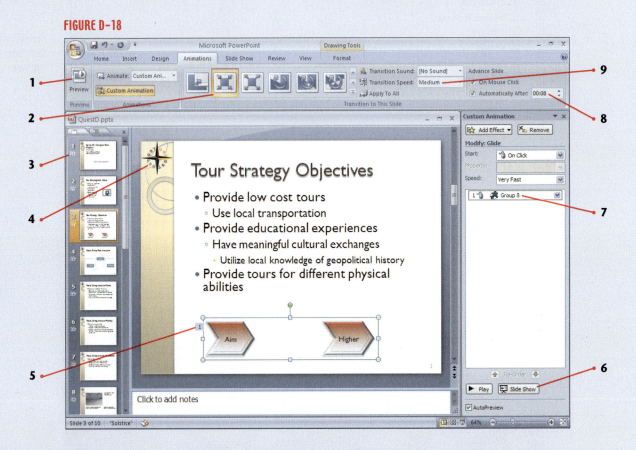

Match each term with the statement that best describes it.

10. Animation tag
11. Background
12. Transitions
13. Masters
14. Metadata
15. Annotate

a. Visual effects that determine how a slide moves in and out of view during a slide show
b. Slides that store theme and placeholder information
c. To draw on a slide during a slide show
d. Includes document properties such as the author's name
e. Identifies the order in which objects are animated
f. The area behind text and graphics

Select the best answer from the list of choices.

16. **Which of the following statements about masters is *not* true?**
    a. Masters store information
    b. Changes made to the slide master are reflected in the handout and notes masters as well
    c. Each slide layout in the presentation has a corresponding slide layout in the Slide Master view
    d. The design theme is placed on the master slide

17. **According to the book, an object placed on the slide master defines which item?**
    a. A background graphic
    b. A logo
    c. A shape
    d. A master placeholder

18. **What is the effect called that determines how a slide moves in and out of view during a slide show?**
    a. Theme
    b. Animation
    c. Timing
    d. Transition

19. **What is the effect called that controls how an object appears on the screen during a slide show?**
    a. Transition
    b. Animation
    c. Path
    d. Template

20. **The Document Inspector can do all of the following *except*,**
    a. look for hidden data
    b. delete metadata
    c. remove on-slide content
    d. locate presentation notes

21. **A PowerPoint file that *can't* be edited or modified defines what type of file?**
    a. A marked as final file
    b. A template file
    c. An inspected file
    d. A file saved in another file format

22. **According to the book, which standard should you follow to evaluate a presentation?**
    a. Slides should include most of the information you wish to present
    b. The message should be outlined in a concise way.
    c. Use many different design elements to keep your audience from getting bored.
    d. Replace visuals with text as often as possible.

23. **Which of the following statements about templates is *not* true?**
    a. The file extension .potx is applied to the PowerPoint file when you save it as a template.
    b. You can create a template from a new presentation.
    c. A template is a type of presentation that contains custom design information.
    d. A template is designed to create custom slide layouts.

▼ SKILLS REVIEW

1. **Understand masters.**
    a. Open the presentation PPT D-3.pptx from the drive and folder where you store your Data Files, then save the presentation as **MediaCom**.
    b. Open the Slide Master view using the View tab, then click the Civic Slide Master thumbnail.
    c. Insert the picture PPT D-4.jpg, then resize the picture so it is 0.8" wide.

    d. Drag the picture to the upper right corner of the slide within the design frame of the slide, then deselect the picture.

    e. Switch to Normal view, then save your changes.

2. Customize the background style.

    a. Switch to Slide 2, click the Design tab, then open the background styles gallery.

    b. Change the background style to Style 3.

    c. Open the Format Background dialog box.

    d. Set the Transparency to 25%, then apply the background to all of the slides.

    e. Close the dialog box, switch to Slide Master view, then open the Civic Slide Master slide.

    f. Select the inserted picture, then use the Picture Tools Format tab to make its background transparent.

    g. Switch to Normal view, then save your changes.

3. Use slide show commands.

    a. Begin the slide show on Slide 1, then proceed to Slide 4.

    b. Use the Felt Tip Pen to circle the words Early Adopters, Mass Adopters, and Late Adopters.

    c. Use the Pen Options menu button to erase all ink on the slide, then change the pointer back to the Arrow.

    d. Right-click the slide and go to Slide 8, use the Highlighter pointer to highlight each bullet on the slide.

    e. Press [Home], then advance through the slide show, don't save any ink annotations, then save your work.

4. Set slide show transitions and timings.

    a. Go to Slide 1, then apply the Wheel Clockwise, 8 Spokes transition in the Wipes group to all of the slides.

    b. Change the transition speed to slow, then switch to Slide Sorter view.

    c. Change the slide timing to 5 seconds, then apply to all of the slides.

    d. Click Slide 10, then apply the Applause sound.

    e. Click Slide 1, then switch to Normal view.

    f. View the slide show, then save your work.

FIGURE D-19: Completed presentation

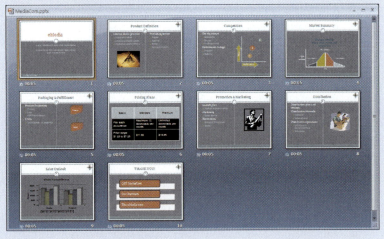

5. Set slide show animation effects.

    a. Go to Slide 2, then open the Custom Animation task pane.

    b. Apply the Emphasis Flash Bulb effect to the title text object, then apply the Entrance Unfold effect to both bulleted text objects.

    c. On Slide 3 apply the Emphasis Shimmer effect to the title text object, then apply the Entrance Rise Up effect to the bulleted text object.

    d. On Slide 4 apply the Entrance Flip effect to the title text object, then apply an Entrance animation effect of your choice from the Exciting group to the six individual objects in the graphic.

    e. Apply animation effects to the rest of the slides in the presentation. Animate all of the text objects and the other objects.

    f. Edit the animations effects as needed, then save your changes.

    g. Compare your presentation to Figure D-19.

6. Inspect a presentation.

   a. Open the Document Properties pane, type **Internet Product** in the Subject text box, then type **Review** in the Status text box

   b. Close the Document Properties pane, then open the Document Inspector dialog box.

   c. Make sure the Off-Slide Content check box is selected, then inspect the presentation.

   d. Delete the off-slide content, and the presentation notes, then close the dialog box.

   e. Save your changes.

7. Evaluate a presentation.

   a. Go to Slide 1, then run a slide show.

   b. Evaluate the presentation using the points described in the lesson as criteria.

   c. Move Slide 6 below Slide 8.

   d. Save your work, then print the slides of your presentation.

8. Create a template.

   a. Save the presentation as a template (.potx) with the name **MediaCom Template** to the drive and folder where your Data Files are stored.

   b. Delete all slides except Slide 1 and Slide 2.

   c. Delete the picture and text on Slide 2, type **Slide Title Here** in the title text placeholder, type **Bulleted List 1** in the left content placeholder, then type **Bulleted List 2** in the right content placeholder.

   d. Delete the subtitle text object on Slide 1, then type **QST MediaCom Template** in the title text object in place of the current text.

   e. Delete the slide transitions and animations on both slides.

   f. Save your work, then print the presentation as handouts, two slides per page.

   g. Close the presentation, then exit PowerPoint.

▼ INDEPENDENT CHALLENGE 1

You are a travel consultant for Turner Travel, located in Portland, Oregon. You have been working on a sales presentation that is going to be accessed by customers on the company Web site. You need to finish up what you have been working on by adding transitions, timings, and animation effects to the sales presentation.

   a. Open the file PPT D-5.pptx from the drive and folder where you store your Data Files, and save the presentation as **TurnerTravel**.

   b. Add your name as the footer on all slides and handouts.

   c. Apply the Fade Through Black slide transitions to all of the slides.

   d. Apply the Entrance Glide animation to the title text on each slide.

   e. Apply the Emphasis Flicker animation to the bulleted text objects on each slide.

   f. Apply the Entrance Thread animation to the table on Slide 8.

   g. Apply a 10 second slide timing to each slide, then change the transition speed to Medium.

   h. Spell check the presentation, then save it.

   i. View the slide show, and evaluate your presentation. Make changes if necessary.

   j. Print the slides as handouts (six slides per page), then close the presentation, and exit PowerPoint.

▼ INDEPENDENT CHALLENGE 2

You are a development engineer at FarNorth Sports, Inc., an international sports product design company located in Winnipeg, Manitoba, Canada. FarNorth Sports designs and manufactures items such as bike helmets, bike racks, and kayak paddles, and markets these items primarily to countries in North America and Western Europe. You need to finish the work on a quarterly presentation that outlines the progress of the company's newest technologies by adding animations, customizing the background, and using the Document Inspector.

a. Open the file PPT D-6.pptx from the drive and folder where you store your Data Files, and save the presentation as **FarNorth**.

b. Apply an appropriate design theme, then apply a new slide background style. Make sure the new background style is appropriate for the design theme you have chosen.

c. Apply the Box Out slide transition to all slides, then animate the following objects: the text on Slide 2, the clip art object on Slide 3, the table on Slide 4, and the chart on Slide 6. View the slide show to evaluate the effects you added and make adjustments as necessary.

d. Run the Document Inspector with all options selected, identify what items the Document Inspector finds, close the Document Inspector dialog box, then review the slides to find the items.

e. Add a slide at the end of the presentation that identifies the items the Document Inspector found.

f. Run the Document Inspector again and remove all items except the document properties.

Advanced Challenge Exercise

- ■ Click the Rehearse Timings button on the Slide Sorter toolbar.
- ■ Set slide timings for each slide in the presentation.
- ■ Save new slide timings.

g. Add your name as a footer to the handouts, save your work, then run a slide show to evaluate your presentation.

h. Print the presentation as handouts (four slides per page), then close the presentation and exit PowerPoint.

▼ INDEPENDENT CHALLENGE 3

You work for JB & Associates Financial, a full service investment and pension firm. Your boss wants you to create a presentation on small business pension plan options to be published on the company Web site. You have completed adding the information to the presentation, now you need to add a design theme, format some information, add some animation effects, and add slide timings.

a. Open the file PPT D-7.pptx from the drive and folder where you store your Data Files, and save the presentation as **SBPlans**.

b. Apply an appropriate design theme.

c. Apply animation effects to the following objects: the shapes on Slide 3 and the text and clip art on Slide 5. View the slide show to evaluate the effects you added and make adjustments as necessary.

d. Convert the text on Slide 4 to a Basic Radial SmartArt graphic (Found in the Cycle category).

e. Apply the Polished style to the SmartArt graphic, then change the colors of the graphic to Colorful Range – Accent Colors 2 to 3

f. Switch to Slide 3, align the Sector and Quality arrow shapes to one another, then align the Allocation and Maturity arrow shapes to one another.

g. Adjust the aligned arrow shapes so they are centered on the Buy/Sell oval shape, then apply a 15 second timing to Slides 3–7 and a 5 second timing to Slides 1 and 2.

Advanced Challenge Exercise

- Open the Slide Master view, select the last slide layout, then click the Insert Layout button.
- Click the Insert Placeholder button arrow, click Table, then drag a placeholder in the blank area of the master slide layout. (*Hint*: Draw the table placeholder so it takes up most of the blank space in the layout.)
- Return to Normal view, apply the new Custom Layout to Slides 6 and 7. Adjust the placeholder in Slide Master view if necessary.

h. Add your name as a footer to the handouts, save your work, then run a slide show to evaluate your presentation.

i. Print the presentation as handouts (four slides per page), then close the presentation and exit PowerPoint.

▼ REAL LIFE INDEPENDENT CHALLENGE

You work for the operations supervisor at the Southern State University student union. Create a presentation that you can eventually publish to the college Web site that describes all of the services offered at the student union.

a. Plan and create the slide presentation that describes the services and events offered at the student union. To help create content, use the student union at your school or use the Internet to locate information on college student unions. The presentation should contain at least six slides.

b. Use an appropriate design theme.

c. Add clip art and photographs available in the Clip Organizer to help create visual interest.

d. Save the presentation as **SSU Services** to the drive and folder where you store your Data Files. View the slide show and evaluate the contents of your presentation. Make any necessary adjustments.

e. Add transitions, animation effects, and timings to the presentation. View the slide show again to evaluate the effects you added.

f. Add your name as a footer to the handouts. Spell check, save, inspect, and print the presentation as handouts (four slides per page). Compare your finished presentation to Figure D-20.

g. Create a template from this presentation. Delete unnecessary slides and objects, type appropriate sample text if necessary, then save the presentation as **SSU Services Template** to the drive and folder where you store your Data Files.

h. Close the presentation and exit PowerPoint.

FIGURE D-20

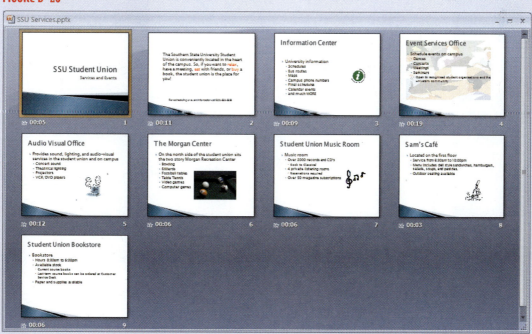

▼ VISUAL WORKSHOP

Open the file PPT D-8.pptx, then save the presentation as a template (.potx) with the filename **Island Travel Template** to the drive and folder where you store your Data Files. Change the presentation to look like Figures D-21 and D-22. Be sure to remove all unnecessary information, objects, and slides from the template presentation. Add your name as a footer to the slides.

FIGURE D-21

FIGURE D-22

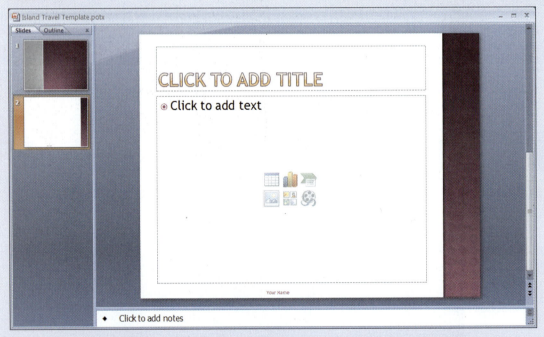

Restoring Defaults in Windows Vista and Disabling and Enabling Windows Aero

Windows Vista is the most recent version of the Windows operating system. An operating system controls the way you work with your computer, supervises running programs, and provides tools for completing your computing tasks. After surveying millions of computer users, Microsoft incorporated their suggestions to make Windows Vista secure, reliable, and easy to use. In fact, Windows Vista is considered the most secure version of Windows yet. Other improvements include a powerful new search feature that lets you quickly search for files and programs from the Start menu and most windows, tools that simplify accessing the Internet, especially with a wireless connection, and multimedia programs that let you enjoy, share, and organize music, photos, and recorded TV. Finally, Windows Vista offers lots of visual appeal with its transparent, three-dimensional design in the Aero experience. This appendix explains how to make sure you are using the Windows Vista default settings for appearance, personalization, security, hardware, and sound and to enable and disable Windows Aero. For more information on Windows Aero, go to *www.microsoft.com/windowsvista/experiences/aero.mspx*.

OBJECTIVES

Restore the defaults in the Appearance and Personalization section

Restore the defaults in the Security section

Restore the defaults in the Hardware and Sound section

Disable Windows Aero

Enable Windows Aero

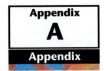

Restoring the Defaults in the Appearance and Personalization Section

The following instructions require a default Windows Vista Ultimate installation and the student logged in with an Administrator account. All of the following settings can be changed by accessing the Control Panel.

STEPS

- **To restore the defaults in the Personalization section**

  1. Click Start, and then click Control Panel. Click Appearance and Personalization, click Personalization, and then compare your screen to Figure A-1

  2. In the Personalization window, click Windows Color and Appearance, select the Default color, and then click OK

  3. In the Personalization window, click Mouse Pointers. In the Mouse Properties dialog box, on the Pointers tab, select Windows Aero (system scheme) in the Scheme drop-down list, and then click OK

  4. In the Personalization window, click Theme. Select Windows Vista from the Theme drop-down list, and then click OK

  5. In the Personalization window, click Display Settings. In the Display Settings dialog box, drag the Resolution bar to 1024 by 768 pixels, and then click OK

FIGURE A-1

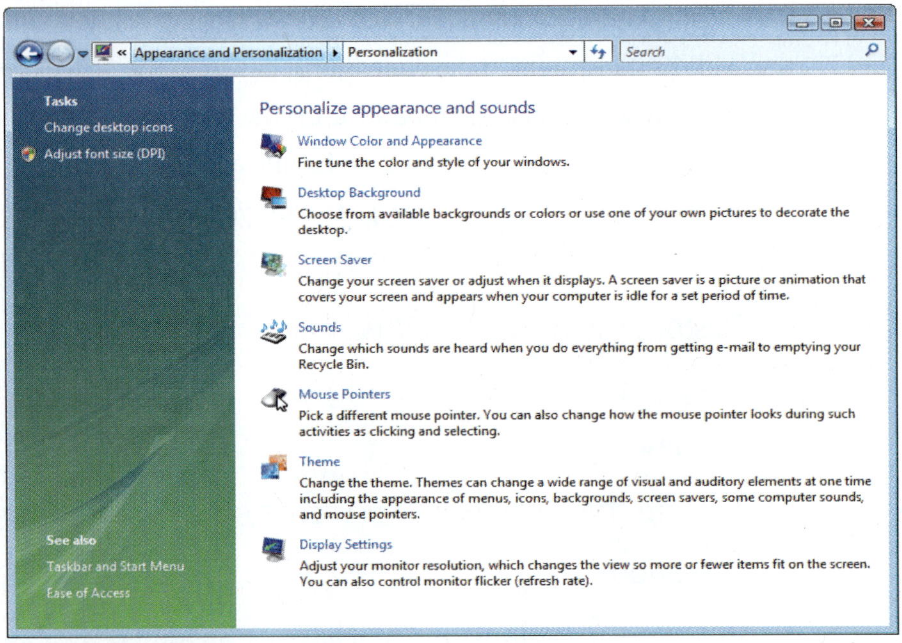

« Appearance and Personalization ► Personalization ▼ 🔍 Search	

Tasks
Change desktop icons
Adjust font size (DPI)

Personalize appearance and sounds

Window Color and Appearance
Fine tune the color and style of your windows.

Desktop Background
Choose from available backgrounds or colors or use one of your own pictures to decorate the desktop.

Screen Saver
Change your screen saver or adjust when it displays. A screen saver is a picture or animation that covers your screen and appears when your computer is idle for a set period of time.

Sounds
Change which sounds are heard when you do everything from getting e-mail to emptying your Recycle Bin.

Mouse Pointers
Pick a different mouse pointer. You can also change how the mouse pointer looks during such activities as clicking and selecting.

Theme
Change the theme. Themes can change a wide range of visual and auditory elements at one time including the appearance of menus, icons, backgrounds, screen savers, some computer sounds, and mouse pointers.

See also
Taskbar and Start Menu
Ease of Access

Display Settings
Adjust your monitor resolution, which changes the view so more or fewer items fit on the screen. You can also control monitor flicker (refresh rate).

- **To restore the defaults in the Taskbar and Start Menu section**
  1. Click Start, and then click Control Panel. Click Appearance and Personalization, click Taskbar and Start Menu, and then compare your screen to Figure A-2
  2. In the Taskbar and Start Menu Properties dialog box, on the Taskbar tab, click to select all checkboxes except for "Auto-hide the taskbar"
  3. On the Start Menu tab, click to select the Start menu radio button and check all items in the Privacy section
  4. In the System icons section on the Notification Area tab, click to select all of the checkboxes except for "Power"
  5. On the Toolbars tab, click to select Quick Launch, none of the other items should be checked
  6. Click OK to close the Taskbar and Start Menu Properties dialog box

- **To restore the defaults in the Folder Options section**
  1. Click Start, and then click Control Panel. Click Appearance and Personalization, click Folder Options, and then compare your screen to Figure A-3
  2. In the Folder Options dialog box, on the General tab, click to select Show preview and filters in the Tasks section, click to select Open each folder in the same window in the Browse folders section, and click to select Double-click to open an item (single-click to select) in the Click items as follows section
  3. On the View tab, click the Reset Folders button, and then click Yes in the Folder views dialog box. Then click the Restore Defaults button
  4. On the Search tab, click the Restore Defaults button
  5. Click OK to close the Folder Options dialog box

- **To restore the defaults in the Windows Sidebar Properties section**
  1. Click Start, and then click Control Panel. Click Appearance and Personalization, click Windows Sidebar Properties, and then compare your screen to Figure A-4
  2. In the Windows Sidebar Properties dialog box, on the Sidebar tab, click to select Start Sidebar when Windows starts. In the Arrangement section, click to select Right, and then click to select 1 in the Display Sidebar on monitor drop-down list
  3. Click OK to close the Windows Sidebar Properties dialog box

FIGURE A-3

FIGURE A-4

FIGURE A-2

Restoring the Defaults in the Security Section

The following instructions require a default Windows Vista Ultimate installation and the student logged in with an Administrator account. All of the following settings can be changed by accessing the Control Panel.

STEPS

- **To restore the defaults in the Windows Firewall section**
    1. Click Start, and then click Control Panel. Click Security, click Windows Firewall, and then compare your screen to Figure A-5
    2. In the Windows Firewall dialog box, click Change settings. If the User Account Control dialog box appears, click Continue
    3. In the Windows Firewall Settings dialog box, click the Advanced tab. Click Restore Defaults, then click Yes in the Restore Defaults Confirmation dialog box
    4. Click OK to close the Windows Firewall Settings dialog box, and then close the Windows Firewall window

- **To restore the defaults in the Internet Options section**
    1. Click Start, and then click Control Panel. Click Security, click Internet Options, and then compare your screen to Figure A-6
    2. In the Internet Properties dialog box, on the General tab, click the Use default button. Click the Settings button in the Tabs section, and then click the Restore defaults button in the Tabbed Browsing Settings dialog box. Click OK to close the Tabbed Browsing Settings dialog box
    3. On the Security tab of the Internet Properties dialog box, click to uncheck the Enable Protected Mode checkbox, if necessary. Click the Default level button in the Security level for this zone section. If possible, click the Reset all zones to default level button
    4. On the Programs tab, click the Make default button in the Default web browser button for Internet Explorer, if possible. If Office is installed, Microsoft Office Word should be selected in the HTML editor drop-down list
    5. On the Advanced tab, click the Restore advanced settings button in the Settings section. Click the Reset button in the Reset Internet Explorer settings section, and then click Reset in the Reset Internet Explorer Settings dialog box
    6. Click Close to close the Reset Internet Explorer Settings dialog box, and then click OK to close the Internet Properties dialog box

FIGURE A-5

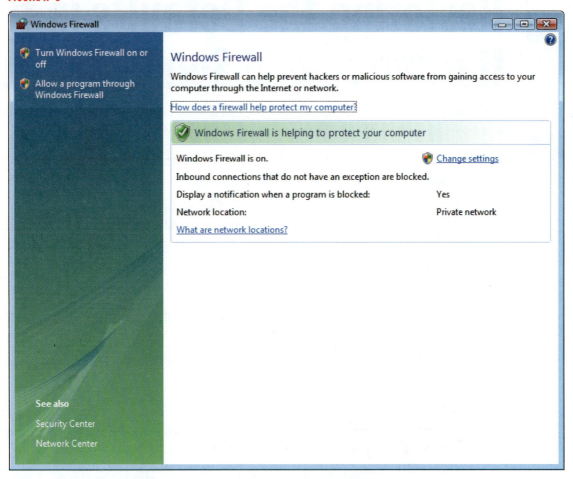

FIGURE A-6

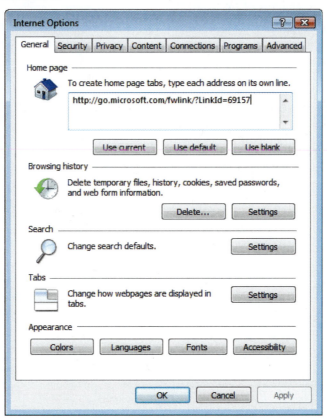

Restoring the Defaults in the Hardware and Sound Section

The following instructions require a default Windows Vista Ultimate installation and the student logged in with an Administrator account. All of the following settings can be changed by accessing the Control Panel.

- **To restore the defaults in the Autoplay section**

  1. Click Start, and then click Control Panel. Click Hardware and Sound, click Autoplay, and then compare your screen to Figure A-7. Scroll down and click the Reset all defaults button in the Devices section at the bottom of the window, and then click Save

- **To restore the defaults in the Sound section**

  1. Click Start, and then click Control Panel. Click Hardware and Sound, click Sound, and then compare your screen to Figure A-8

  2. In the Sound dialog box, on the Sounds tab, select Windows Default from the Sound Scheme drop-down list, and then click OK

- **To restore the defaults in the Mouse section**

  1. Click Start, and then click Control Panel. Click Hardware and Sound, click Mouse, and then compare your screen to Figure A-9

  2. In the Mouse Properties dialog box, on the Pointers tab, select Windows Aero (system scheme) from the Scheme drop-down list

  3. Click OK to close the Mouse Properties dialog box

FIGURE A-7

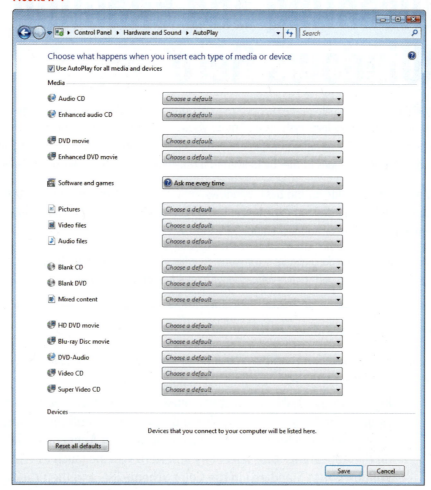

FIGURE A-8

FIGURE A-9

Disabling and Enabling Windows Aero

Unlike prior versions of Windows, Windows Vista provides two distinct user interface experiences: a "basic" experience for entry-level systems and more visually dynamic experience called Windows Aero. Both offer a new and intuitive navigation experience that helps you more easily find and organize your applications and files, but Aero goes further by delivering a truly next-generation desktop experience.

Windows Aero builds on the basic Windows Vista user experience and offers Microsoft's best-designed, highest-performing desktop experience. Using Aero requires a PC with compatible graphics adapter and running a Premium or Business edition of Windows Vista.

The following instructions require a computer capable of running Windows Aero, with a default Windows Vista Ultimate installation and student logged in with an Administrator account.

STEPS

- **To Disable Windows Aero**

We recommend that students using this book disable Windows Aero and restore their operating systems default settings (instructions to follow).

1. **Right-click the desktop, select Personalize, and then compare your screen in Figure A-10. Select Window Color and Appearance, and then select Open classic appeareance properties for more color options. In Appearance Settings dialog box, on the Appearance tab, select any non-Aero scheme (such as Windows Vista Basic or Windows Vista Standard) in the Color Scheme list, and then click OK. Figure A-11 compares Windows Aero to other color schemes. Note that this book uses Windows Vista Basic as the color scheme**

- **To Enable Windows Aero**

1. **Right-click the desktop, and then select Personalize. Select Window Color and Appearance, then select Windows Aero in the Color scheme list, and then click OK in the Appearance Settings dialog box**

FIGURE A-10

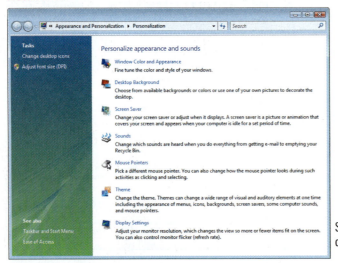

Select other color schemes

FIGURE A-11

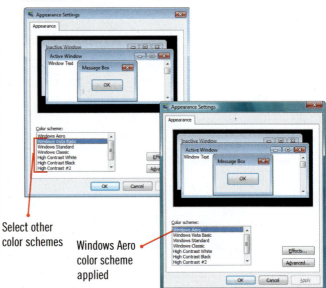

Windows Aero color scheme applied

Glossary

Active The currently available document, program, or object; on the taskbar, the button of the active document is appears in a darker shade while the buttons of other open documents are dimmed.

Active cell A selected cell in an Excel worksheet.

Adjustment handle A small yellow diamond that changes the appearance of an object's most prominent feature.

Align To place objects' edges or centers on the same plane.

Animation tag Identifies the order an object is animated on a slide during a slide show.

Annotate A freehand drawing on the screen made by using the Annotation tool. You can annotate only in Slide Show view.

Axis label Text in a worksheet that identifies data.

.bmp The abbreviation for the bitmap graphics file format.

Background The area behind the text and graphics on a slide.

Background graphic An object placed on the slide master.

Backward-compatible Software feature that enables documents saved in an older version of a program to be opened in a newer version of the program.

Category axis The horizontal axis in a chart.

Cell The intersection of a column and row in a worksheet, datasheet, or table.

Chart A graphical representation of numerical data from a worksheet. Types include 2-D and 3-D column, bar, pie, area, and line charts.

Clip art Predesigned graphic images you can insert in any document or presentation to enhance its appearance.

Clip Organizer A library of art, pictures, sounds, video clips, and animations that all Office applications share.

Clipboard Temporary storage area in Windows.

Column heading The gray box containing the column letter at the top of the column in a worksheet.

Compatible The capability of different programs to work together and exchange data.

Content placeholder A placeholder that is used to enter text or objects such as clip art, charts, or pictures.

Contextual tab Tab on the Ribbon that appears when needed to complete a specific task; for example, if you select a chart on a PowerPoint slide, three contextual Chart Tool tabs (Design, Layout, and Format) appear.

Crop To hide part of an object, such as clip art using the Cropping tool or to delete a part of a picture.

Data series A column or row in a datasheet.

Data series marker A graphical representation of a data series, such as a bar or column.

Dialog box A window that opens when a program needs more information to carry out a command.

Dialog box launcher An icon available in many groups on the Ribbon that you can click to open a dialog box or task pane, offering an alternative way to choose commands.

Digital Signature A way to authenticate a presentation file using computer cryptography. A digital signature is not visible in a presentation.

Distribute To evenly divide the space horizontally or vertically between objects relative to each other or the slide edges.

Document Inspector A PowerPoint feature that examines a presentation for hidden data or personal information.

Document window Workspace in the program window that displays the current presentation or document.

Embedded object An object that is created in one application and inserted to another. Embedded objects remain connected to the original program file in which they were created for easy editing.

File The presentation you create using PowerPoint. An electronic collection of stored data that has a unique name, distinguishing it from other files.

Group To combine multiple objects into one object on a slide

Group (Ribbon) A set of like commands on each tab of the Ribbon.

Insertion point A blinking vertical line that indicates where the next character will appear when text is entered in a text placeholder in PowerPoint.

Integrate To incorporate a document and parts of a document created in one program into another program; for example, to incorporate an Excel chart into a PowerPoint slide, or an Access table into a Word document.

Interface The look and feel of a program; for example, the appearance of commands and the way they are organized in the program window.

Launch To open or start a program on your computer.

Legend Names in the top row of a worksheet that provides information about the data.

Live Preview A feature that lets you point to a choice in a gallery or palette and see the results in the document before you apply the change.

Masters One of three views that stores information about the presentation theme, fonts, placeholders, and other background objects. The three views are Slide Master view, Handout Master view, and Notes Master view.

Metadata Another name for document properties that includes the author name, the document subject, the document title, and other personal information.

Microsoft Graph A program that creates a chart to graphically depict numerical information when you don't have access to Microsoft Excel.

Mini toolbar A small toolbar that appears next to selected text.

Normal view A presentation view that divides the presentation window into three sections: Slides or Outline tab, Slide pane, and Notes pane.

Notes Page view A presentation view that displays a reduced image of the current slide above a large text box where you can type notes.

Notes pane The area in Normal view that shows speaker notes for the current slide; also in Notes Page view, the area below the slide image that contains speaker notes.

Object An item you place or draw on a slide that can be modified. Objects include drawn lines and shapes, text, clip art, imported pictures, and charts.

Online collaboration The ability to incorporate feedback or share information across the Internet or a company network or intranet.

Outline tab The section in Normal view that displays your presentation text in the form of an outline, without graphics.

Pane A section of the PowerPoint window, such as the Slide or Notes pane.

Picture A digital photograph, piece of line art, or clip art that is created in another program and is inserted into PowerPoint.

Placeholder A dashed line box where you place text or objects.

PowerPoint Viewer A special application designed to run a PowerPoint slide show on any compatible computer that does not have PowerPoint installed.

PowerPoint window A window that contains the running PowerPoint application. The PowerPoint window includes the Ribbon, the panes, and Presentation window.

Program tab Single tab on the Ribbon specific to a particular view, such as Print Preview.

Presentation software A software program used to organize and present information.

Preview Prior to printing, to see onscreen exactly how the printed presentation will look.

Quick Access toolbar A small customizable toolbar at the top of the PowerPoint window that contains buttons for commonly used Office commands such as Save and Undo.

Quick Style Determines how fonts, colors, and effects of the theme are combined and which color, font, and effect is dominant. A quick style can be applied to Smart Art, shapes, or text.

Read-only A file that can't be edited or modified.

Ribbon A wide (toolbar-like) band that runs across the PowerPoint window that organizes primary commands into tabs and groups.

Rotate handle A green circular handle at the top of a selected object that you can drag to rotate the selected object.

Row heading The gray box containing the row number to the left of the row in a worksheet.

Scale To change the size of a graphic to a specific percentage of its original size.

Screen capture A snapshot of your screen, as if you took a picture of it with a camera, which you can paste into a document or presentation.

Selection box A dashed border that appears around a text object or placeholder, indicating that it is ready to accept text.

Series in Columns The information in the columns of a worksheet that are on the Value axis; the row labels are on the Category axis.

Series in Rows The information in the rows of a worksheet that are on the Value axis; the column labels are on the Category axis.

Sizing handles The small circles and squares that appear around a selected object. Dragging a sizing handle resizes the object.

Slide layout This determines how all of the elements on a slide are arranged, including text and content placeholders.

Slide pane The section of Normal view that contains the current slide.

Slide Show view A view that shows a presentation as an electronic slide show; each slide fills the screen.

Slide Sorter view A view that displays a thumbnail of all slides in the order in which they appear in your presentation; used to rearrange slides and slide transitions.

Slides tab The section in Normal View that displays the slides of your presentation as small thumbnails.

Slide timing The amount of time a slide is visible on the screen during a slide show.

Slide transition The special effect that moves one slide off the screen and the next slide on the screen during a slide show. Each slide can have its own transition effect.

SmartArt A professional quality graphic diagram that visually illustrates text.

SmartArt Style A pre-set combination of formatting options that follows the design theme that you can apply to a SmartArt graphic.

Status bar The bar at the bottom of the PowerPoint window that contains messages about what you are doing and seeing in PowerPoint, such as the current slide number or the current theme.

Subtitle text placeholder A box on the title slide reserved for subpoint text.

Suite A group of programs that are bundled together and share a similar interface, making it easy to transfer skills and program content among them.

Tab A set of commands on the Ribbon related to a common set of tasks or features. Tabs are further organized into groups of related commands.

Task pane A separate pane that contains sets of menus, lists, options, and hyperlinks such as the Custom Animation task pane that are used to customize objects.

Template A type of presentation that contains custom design information made to the slide master, slide layouts, and theme.

Text label A text box you create using the Text Box button, where the text does not automatically wrap inside the box. Text box text does not appear in the Outline tab.

Text placeholder A box with a dotted border and text that you replace with your own text.

Theme Predesigned combinations of colors, fonts, effects, and formatting attributes you can apply to a presentation or any document in any Office program.

Theme colors The set of 12 coordinated colors that make up a PowerPoint presentation; a color scheme assigns colors for text, lines, fills, accents, hyperlinks, and background.

Thumbnail A small image of a slide. Thumbnails are visible on the Slides tab and in Slide Sorter view.

Title The first line or heading on a slide.

Title bar Area at the top of every program window that displays the document and program name.

Title placeholder A box on a slide reserved for the title of a presentation or slide.

Title slide The first slide in a presentation.

User interface A collective term for all the ways you interact with a software program.

Value axis The vertical axis in a chart.

View A way of displaying a presentation, such as Normal view, Notes Page view, Slide Sorter view, and Slide Show view. Also, display settings that show or hide selected elements of a document in the document window, to make it easier to focus on a certain task, such as formatting or reading text.

View Shortcuts The buttons at the bottom of the PowerPoint window that you click to switch among views.

Window A rectangular area of the screen where you view and work on the open file.

WordArt A set of decorative styles or text effects that is applied to text.

Word processing box A text box you create using the Text Box button, where the text automatically wraps inside the box.

Worksheet The document in Microsoft Excel that stores data in cells. Used to create a chart in PowerPoint.

Zooming in A feature that makes a document appear bigger but shows less of it on screen at once; does not affect actual document size.

Zooming out A feature that shows more of a document on screen at once but at a reduced size; does not affect actual document size.

Zoom slider A feature that allows you to change the zoom percentage of a slide. Located in the status bar.

Index